I0161281

RichThoughts for Breakfast

Volume 3

Harold Herring

President of The Debt Free Army
& RichThoughts TV

www.HaroldHerring.com

Debt Free Army
PO Box 900000, Fort Worth, TX 76161

RichThoughts for Breakfast Volume 3
by Harold Herring

ISBN 978-0-9763668-3-6

PO Box 900000, Fort Worth, TX 76161
817-222-0011
harold@haroldherring.com

Unless otherwise noted, Scripture references are taken from the King James Version of the Bible.

Printed in the United States of America.

RichThoughts for Breakfast
Volume 3

Table of Contents

Day 1

Freedom Over What's Familiar

God stirred me to place the following post on Facebook:

> "*Always remember this day. This is the day when you came out of Egypt from a house of slavery. God brought you out of here with a powerful hand ...*" (Exodus 13:3, the Message Bible).

Decide now that you will no longer be a slave to the moneylenders (Proverbs 22:7) ... today begins your financial deliverance.

In Egypt, the children of God were told where to live; where to work; what they could eat, and when they could eat it; where they could go, and what they could do; and they suffered hardship, persecution and lack.

In Egypt, the children of God were slaves who were not in control of their own destiny.

But then ... **God set the captives free.**

The children of Israel left Egypt ... free to go where they wanted; so they could worship Jehovah God while walking in divine health ... never needing to buy clothes.

The children of Israel left Egypt … to fulfill God's prophecy to His chosen people; loaded down with all the gold and jewels they could carry; free to manifest the promises of God in their lives; no longer bound to the chains of slavery in the natural.

You would think the children of Israel would have been happy … shouting "Hallelujah" while embracing the promise of a land flowing with milk and honey. They left the bondage of slavery on a journey to freedom and luxury … but they weren't happy.

The children of Israel had personally witnessed the plagues God brought upon the Egyptians. They experienced how God provided for them in the wilderness ... how He had destroyed Pharaoh's army ... yet they murmured and complained.

The children of Israel even wanted to return to Egypt!

They wanted to return to all they'd left behind ... everything that had held them in bondage ... to the land of never enough.

It's amazing to many of us that those who were now free, prosperous and healthy would willingly trade that lifestyle for the feel of the whips from the cruel taskmasters.

It's easy to condemn the children of Israel for desiring to go back into slavery.

May I suggest that it wasn't the slavery that was attractive to them but the familiarity of what to expect.

There are five reasons a person will trade freedom for the slavery of what's familiar.

1. **Some people choose what's familiar because it's easier than moving out and facing the unknown.**

They will live with what's familiar even though it may be less than what's desirable. They like the familiar feel of living in a comfort zone.

2. **Some people choose what's familiar because it's all they've ever known.**

They've never heard or understood that they have the ability to move beyond what's been the norm in their lives. They've never been told or come to understand there are no limitations to their future success.

3. **Some people choose what's familiar because their mental hard drive responds more to fear than faith.**

This comes from a lack of biblical insight into God's benefit package.

4. **Some people choose what's familiar because ... because they're too lazy to change.**

It's a fairly safe bet to say that people who are lazy have never read the book of Proverbs. I should point out that there are some people who work hard with their hands, but they're mentally lazy in their quest for knowledge or self-improvement. They choose to live in mediocrity instead of choosing excellence.

5. Some people choose what's familiar to them because of their own self-image.

These folks haven't yet caught a glimpse of who they are in Christ nor have they come to the realization that nothing is impossible to them. They say, "I'm a slave ... that's all I know how to do," or, "I'm in debt ... we've always been in debt ... and there's nothing I can do to change that." **It's the lie the devil feeds some Christians, and sadly, they buy into it.**

Here's the bottom line: **You will never be all that God wants you to be ... if you always settle for what's familiar ... what's comfortable ... and you are afraid to move forward.**

A person who chooses this path in life will become a slave to the ordinary ... never tasting the land flowing with milk and honey that God has promised them ... always walking in the familiar ... and never seeking the good life that He has promised all His children.

As I said, there are those who seek the path of least resistance in life ... those who never want to try anything new ... who are totally comfortable with what's familiar to them ... even if it's to their own disadvantage.

That's the trouble with way too many believers ... they settle for a life of mediocrity rather than daring to take a step of faith ... to move outside their comfort zone ... to embrace the invisible in order to achieve the seemingly impossible.

God brought His children out of Israel for a purpose and with a promise. He wants to do the same thing for you.

He wants you to realize that you were created for a purpose, and it wasn't to live your days in debt and lack.

God wants you to embrace, expect and experience every one of His precious promises for you ... but you'll never receive all He has if you want to return to Egypt. His principles ... His precepts will have to replace the slave mentality of living in debt.

Sadly, there are some believers who get out of debt ... only to get right back into debt once again. Why? **Because debt and monthly payments are familiar to them ... they lack the discipline to fight off the devil's deceptions.**

I can't tell you the number of people who've told me that they use our material to become debt free ... only to allow themselves back into the creditor's grip of debt.

God wants every person reading my words today ... to cast off the shackles of debt and bondage ... quit being "... a slave to the moneylenders." (Proverbs 22:7 in the Contemporary English Version)

God has empowered you to cast off all those shackles

that have you bound so you can move into total freedom. The reality is that you will never be truly free until you are financially free.

To move in this freedom ... you've got to stop looking back ... you've got to realize that debt is no longer an option. What you tolerate, you accept.

You have to move outside your comfort zone ... that which is familiar to you ... to gain control of your spending ... to create your own personalized out-of-debt plan.

How do you overcome the allure of what's familiar ... how do you get past debt and payments to move into your promised land of financial freedom?

First, see yourself the way God sees you ... debt free and moving in His abundant provision.

Second, break the habit of spending money in familiar places. Make the change in your financial lifestyle to accommodate your desire ... your commitment to financial freedom.

Third, celebrate every advance you make against the devil of debt. Take pride in breaking free of what's familiar as you shake off the chains of debt and bondage.

Finally, grab hold of scriptures that will strengthen and minister to you in your journey through the wilderness of financial despair into your promised land of financial independence.

Let me close this teaching with the words found in Galatians 5:1 in the Message Bible:

> *"Christ has set us free to live a free life. So take your stand! Never again let anyone put a harness of slavery on you."*

Leave Egypt behind ... get out of financial bondage ... out of what's been familiar to you ... set your eyes on a journey to the debt-free lifestyle ... don't look back ... press toward your prize of true and lasting freedom. **Even as you cross the desert ... the Promised Land is straight ahead.**

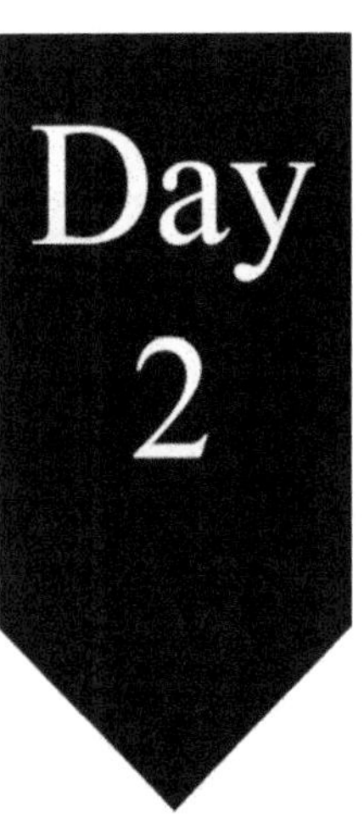

You've Been Down, but You're Coming Up

The Lord directed me to encourage you ... in whatever adversity you might be facing. He wants me to tell you that you may have been down ... but you're definitely coming up.

No matter how far you've been down or what evil has come against you ... God will bring you up and out.

Proverbs 24:15, 16 in the Message Bible warns anyone who comes against His own:

> *"Don't interfere with good people's lives; don't try to get the best of them. No matter how many times you trip them up, God-loyal people don't stay down long; Soon they're up on their feet, while the wicked end up flat on their faces."*

Do you remember the story of Naaman, the Commander of the Syrian Army? He had leprosy and thought he was going to die, but God had other plans.

Let's read a portion of the passage from 2 Kings 5:1-14 in the New Living Translation.

In this passage, Naaman was the commander of his army.

He was a mighty warrior, and still, he suffered from leprosy.

> *"A young girl ... had been given to Naaman's wife as a maid. One day the girl said to her mistress, 'I wish my master would go to see the prophet in Samaria. He would heal him of his leprosy.'*
>
> *"So Naaman told the king what the young girl from Israel had said. 'Go and visit the prophet,' the king of Aram told him. 'I will send a letter of introduction for you to take to the king of Israel.'*
>
> *"So Naaman started out, carrying as gifts 750 pounds of silver, 150 pounds of gold, and ten sets of clothing ..."*

At today's prices he carried over $400,000 in silver ... plus $4,000,000 in gold and $20,000 in Armani suits.

> *"So Naaman went with his horses and chariots and waited at the door of Elisha's house. But Elisha sent a messenger out to him with this message:* ***'Go and wash yourself seven times in the Jordan River. Then your skin will be restored, and you will be healed of your leprosy.****'*
>
> *"But Naaman became angry and stalked away. 'I thought he would certainly come out to meet me!' he said. 'I expected him to wave his hand over the leprosy and call on the name of the Lord his God and heal me! Aren't the rivers of Damascus, the Abana and the Pharpar, better than any of the*

> *rivers of Israel? Why shouldn't I wash in them and be healed?' So Naaman turned and went away in a rage.*
>
> *"But his officers tried to reason with him and said, 'Sir, if the prophet had told you to do something very difficult, wouldn't you have done it? So you should certainly obey him when he says simply, "Go and wash and be cured!" ' So Naaman went down to the Jordan River and dipped himself seven times, as the man of God had instructed him. And his skin became as healthy as the skin of a young child's, and he was healed!"*

While reading this account about Naaman, **God showed me seven powerful principles for everyone who's faced difficult, seemingly impossible problems.**

1. Accept what the man of God says ...

2 Kings 5:11 in the New Living Translation says:

> *"But Naaman became angry and stalked away. 'I thought he would certainly come out to meet me!' he said. 'I expected him to wave his hand over the leprosy and call on the name of the Lord his God and heal me!' "*

There are defining moments in our lives when God uses a man or woman under His influence to speak a Word into our lives ... we need to listen to what they have to say ... regardless of how seemingly ridiculous it may sound ... and especially if it's a word of correction.

2. **Put your pride aside.**

In 2 Kings 5:11 ... Naaman is saying, "Doesn't this prophet know who I am ... and who is he to treat me this way?"

It's always important to remember that pride leads to sin and problems.

Proverbs 13:10 says:

> *"Only by pride cometh contention: but with the well advised is wisdom."*

Dwight L. Moody the great evangelist once said: **"Be humble or you'll stumble."**

One of the most painful falls people face is when they trip over their own egos.

3. **Forget what everyone else thinks.**

No doubt Naaman was wondering what his servants would think ... what passersby would think ... what people would think about a man of his stature dunking himself in such a dirty river.

Are we more concerned about looking ridiculous or obeying the man, word or voice of God?

No one else can fight your battles ... no one else will answer for your obedience to God's directions or lack thereof on judgment day ... no one else can walk in your shoes ... but you.

Here's a revelation ... **<u>what someone else "thinks" ... will do nothing to change your circumstances ... but you are the one who can make that change</u>.**

4. <u>Ignore your circumstances</u>.

What would have happened if Naaman had given up after dipping himself once in the River Jordan? He would still have had leprosy.

If Naaman had given up before going down the seventh time ... he would have never been free of leprosy.

Neither his reputation, his position in the Syrian government, or his money could deliver him ... but His complete obedience to the man of God ... saved his life.

How many times has God told you to sow a specific seed and you did ... but when you didn't receive an immediate harvest or financial deliverance, you either doubted His direction, questioned your gift or hesitated the next time He directed you to sow?

There are believers who've stopped tithing and giving because of their circumstances ... when that's the absolute worst time to stop. Why ignore the only guaranteed solution to all your financial problems?

5. <u>Wash away your sins/past</u>.

Let's look at 2 Kings 5:14 one more time:

"Then went he down, and dipped himself seven

> *times in Jordan, according to the saying of the man of God: and his flesh came again like unto the flesh of a little child, and he was clean."*

The stain of leprosy was washed away ... his skin was as fresh and pure as that of a little child. He was clean from the top of his head to the soles of his feet.

When you and I confess our sins ... give our hearts to Jesus ... then the stain of all our sins is washed away.

6. **Don't quit—or give up when it looks like all is lost.**

Naaman, who already had his pride wounded, could have quit after going down the first, second, third, fourth, fifth or sixth time ... but he didn't ... and his obedience to the man of God brought his deliverance.

If Naaman had quit ... he never would have experienced miracle manifestation.

Psalm 27:13 in the Message Bible says:

> *"I'm sure now I'll see God's goodness in the exuberant earth. Stay with God! Take heart. Don't quit. I'll say it again: Stay with God."*

That's a word for you this day … DON'T QUIT … your miracle breakthrough is at hand.

7. **Receive the victory.**

Naaman lost more than his leprosy in the River Jordan ... he lost his need for pride, because he found something even more powerful than a clean bill of health.

2 Kings 5:15 in the Amplified Bible says:

> *"Then Naaman returned to the man of God, he and all his company, and stood before him. He said, Behold, now I know that there is no God in all the earth but in Israel ..."*

He found the only true and living God.

You may have been down ... due a lack of retirement or investment income ... but you're coming up.

You may have been down ... due to foreclosure and eviction ... but you're coming up.

You may have been down ... due to an attack on your health ... but you're coming up.

You may have been down ... due to a mountain of bills ... but you're coming up.

You may have been down ... due to your spouse or children being lost ... but you're coming up.

You may have been down ... due to your addiction to something other than the Word of God ... but you're coming up.

There's nothing wrong with being down, out and wrong ... as long as you're ready to get up, right and in.

Order Out of Chaos

Do you ever feel your life is a bit chaotic?

Allow God to bring order out of any chaos, financial or otherwise, that you've been dealing with. **God is the master of organization.**

In the first twenty words of Genesis we find the earth is *"... formless and empty, darkness was over the surface of the deep ..."* (Genesis 1:2)

Next we read where the Spirit of God moves across the earth. Before the end of the 46th word in Genesis we read in Chapter 1:3 where God said:

> *"... Let there be light, and there was light."*

God is an organizer ... He brings order and light out of chaos and darkness.

Do you need order brought into your finances?

Do you need order brought into your workplace environment?

Do you need order brought into every situation you're

dealing with right now?

There are seven ways to bring order out of chaos.

1. **We must recognize that chaos, confusion and lack of order are of the devil.**

Where you find sin ... you find confusion.

2 Chronicles 15:5 in the Contemporary English Version says:

> *"There was so much confusion in those days that it wasn't safe to go anywhere in Israel."*

James 3:16 says:

> *"For where envying and strife is, there is confusion and every evil work."*

2. **When you're living in chaos and confusion ... the change starts ... but it starts with you.**

> Mahatma Gandhi said ...
>
> **"We must be the change that we wish to see in the world."**

- ✓ Your learning environment ... where you study the Word … needs to change.
- ✓ Your living environment ... where you spend your

down time with your family … needs to change.

- ✓ Your preparation environment ... where you get ready for work, i.e., bathroom and closet … needs to change.
- ✓ Your transportation environment ... what you ride in from home to work … needs to change.
- ✓ Your workplace environment ... where you spend at least 8 hours every day … needs to change.
- ✓ Your nourishment environment ... where you eat … needs to change.
- ✓ Your spiritual environment ... where God can bring the change needed in your life … needs to change.

3. God always has a plan to bring order out of any kind of chaos.

The greatest chaos I find facing many Americans is in their personal finances.

If your financial affairs are in disarray, you need to know where you're at before you can develop a plan to come out of debt and into financial freedom.

First, if you're not doing so already, BALANCE YOUR CHECKBOOK.

You must ALWAYS balance your checkbook unless you

fall into the category of the rich J. Paul Getty describes:

"If you can actually count your money, then you're not a rich man."

Second, for the next thirty days you need to write down every single PENNY you spend.

I'm sure you know where the big money goes, but it's most often the little money that adds up to big money.

If you have an iPhone download the free app "Easy Spending Expense Tracker." If you have an Android phone ... download the free app "Expense Tracker." If you don't have a smart phone … use a small spiral ring binder—the kind a man can put in his shirt pocket and a woman can put in her purse.

Assign a category to each entry, such as eating out. If you're married, both spouses should be a part of this process. You know where the big money is going, but you will be amazed at where the small money goes. Once you know where your money is going, then you can redirect funds to your out-of-debt plan.

This may not seem like your kind of fun, but let me tell you that if you want order instead of chaos, it's worth it.

Third, create a plan to get out of debt with a specific timeline for your financial freedom.

Our Master Plan book is a great tool to use.

4. God will raise up a leader to bring order out of chaos and confusion.

Proverbs 28:2 in the Message Bible says:

> *"When the country is in chaos, everybody has a plan to fix it— But it takes a leader of real understanding to straighten things out."*

When God wants something done ... He always gives it to one person to do.

1 Samuel 9:17 in the New Century Version says:

> *"When Samuel first saw Saul, the Lord said to Samuel, 'This is the man I told you about. He will organize my people.' "*

The real question you should ask yourself is ... **are you the one God wants to use to bring order out of certain chaotic situations?**

5. Relax in God … don't panic over your situation, or else the chaos and confusion will increase instead of disappear.

As a believer ... if you're knowledgeable of the Word ... you should never EVER panic.

Deuteronomy 31:6 in the New Living Translation says:

> *"So be strong and courageous! Do not be afraid and do not panic before them. For the Lord your God will personally go ahead of you. He will neither fail you nor abandon you."*

There are actually nine times that the Message Bible says "don't panic." My favorite of those verses is Deuteronomy 20:3-4 which says:

> *"... In a few minutes you're going to do battle with your enemies. Don't waver in resolve. Don't fear. Don't hesitate. Don't panic. God, your God, is right there with you, fighting with you against your enemies, fighting to win."*

6. **Eliminate anything or minimize anyone who is creating chaos and confusion in your life.**

Ephesians 4:20 in the Message Bible says:

> *"But that's no life for you. You learned Christ! My assumption is that you have paid careful attention to him, been well instructed in the truth precisely as we have it in Jesus. Since, then, we do not have the excuse of ignorance, everything—and I do mean everything—connected with that old way of life has to go. It's rotten through and through. Get rid of it! And then take on an entirely new way of life—a God-fashioned life, a life renewed from the inside*

> *and working itself into your conduct as God accurately reproduces his character in you."*

Sadly, many believers have become addicted to things ... you can't live with one foot in the world and one foot in the Word. God knows what things you need. Control your things … don't let them control you.

Ezekiel 20:7 in the Message Bible says:

> *"At that time I told them, 'Get rid of all the vile things that you've become addicted to. Don't make yourselves filthy with the Egyptian no-god idols. I alone am God, your God.' "*

7. Pay attention, do what I say and watch order flow from chaos and confusion.

You are the one person who has allowed chaos and confusion in your life ... now you can make a decision that enough is enough.

If you follow the instructions of the Word ... you will be living an organized life filled with promise. However, if you aren't responsive and obedient to the Word of God ... then you will never totally experience a life worth living.

Hebrews 3:19 in the Message Bible says:

> *"They never got there because they never listened, never believed."*

God is a God of order ... He is the great organizer. In

fact, He planned a Marriage Supper two thousand years before it happened. He knows the end from the beginning. The book of Revelation reveals that.

Allow Him to guide your life from the chaos and confusion you experience now into a rich and satisfying life (John 10:10 in the New Living Translation).

"In a time of drastic change it is the learners who inherit the future. The learned usually find themselves equipped to live in a world that no longer exists."

Eric Hoffer

7 Reasons Why I Love Isaiah 48:17

Have you ever said, "I don't know what to do?"

If so, you don't ever have to say it again.

There is never a reason for any born-again Christian to ever worry or wonder about what to do next.

Isaiah 48:17 says:

> *"Thus saith the LORD, thy Redeemer, the Holy One of Israel; I am the LORD thy God which teacheth thee* ***to profit****, which leadeth thee by the way that thou shouldest go."*

Your loving Heavenly Father will teach you the way you should go. He will show you the path that is of the greatest benefit to you.

The Message Bible translation of Isaiah 48:17 says:

> *"I am God, your God who teaches you how to live right and well. I show you what to do, where to go."*

Let's look at the *7 Reasons Why I Love Isaiah 48:17.*

1. I am God ...

He is the great "I Am." There is no one else like Him in the entire universe.

Isaiah 45:22 says:

> *"Look unto me, and be ye saved, all the ends of the earth: for I am God, and there is none else."*

If you want to begin an interesting study in the Word ... look at each of the 141 verses in the Message Bible where you find the phrase "I am God."

Today I want to share the first time "I am God" is used in the Message Bible. It's found in Genesis 28:13-15:

> *"Then God was right before him, saying, 'I am God, the God of Abraham your father and the God of Isaac ... Yes. I'll stay with you, I'll protect you wherever you go, and I'll bring you back to this very ground.* ***I'll stick with you until I've done everything I promised you.' "***

When the scripture says "I am God," you need to understand ... it's filled with the power of promise.

2. Your God ...

God is not just God ... He's your personal God.

Genesis 17:7 in the New Living Translation says:

> *"I will confirm my covenant with you and your descendants after you, from generation to generation. This is the everlasting covenant: I will always be your God and the God of your descendants after you."*

Your God is there to help you in every situation, circumstance and problem that you face.

Your God will be your deliverer ... and He will always give you the right things to say.

Psalm 81:10 in the New Living Translation says:

> *"For it was I, the Lord your God, who rescued you from the land of Egypt. Open your mouth wide, and I will fill it with good things."*

All your God requires of you is found in Matthew 22:37 in the New Living Translation which says:

> *"Jesus replied, 'You must love the Lord your God with all your heart, all your soul, and all your mind.' "*

Just for the record … the phrase "Your God" appears 473 times in the New Living Translation.

3. Who teaches you …

1 John 2:26 in the Message Bible says:

> *"I've written to warn you about those who are*

> *trying to deceive you.* ***But they're no match for what is embedded deeply within you—Christ's anointing, no less!*** *You don't need any of their so-called teaching. Christ's anointing teaches you the truth on everything you need to know about yourself and him, uncontaminated by a single lie. Live deeply in what you were taught."*

God not only teaches you ... but He has embedded Christ's anointing deeply within you.

I trust you fully comprehend what this scripture is saying to you.

You have the anointing of Christ deep inside you. The verse also says, "*Live deeply in what you were taught."*

Job 22:22 in the New International Reader's Version offers some pretty good advice when it says:

> *"Do what he teaches you to do. Keep his words in your heart."*

4. How to live right …

There should never be any question about what's required of us to live our lives in a right manner before God.

Ezekiel 20:11 in the Contemporary English Version says:

> *"I gave them my laws and teachings, so they would know how to live right."*

Without question, God's Word gives us the specific instructions on how to correct the mistakes that we will inevitably make so we can live right before Him.

2 Timothy 3:16 in the New Century Version says:

> *"All Scripture is inspired by God and is useful for teaching, for showing people what is wrong in their lives, for correcting faults, and for teaching how to live right."*

5. How to live well …

Deuteronomy 4:39 in the Message Bible says:

> *"Know this well, then. Take it to heart right now: God is in Heaven above; God is on Earth below. He's the only God there is. Obediently live by his rules and commands which I'm giving you today so that you'll live well and your children after you—oh, you'll live a long time in the land that God, your God, is giving you."*

A little further into Deuteronomy we're told the key to living well.

Deuteronomy 29:9 in the Message Bible says:

> *"Diligently keep the words of this Covenant. Do what they say so that you will live well and wisely in every detail."*

Obey His Word … or as I like to say it … **Read your**

Bible … do what it says.

Why does He want us to live well? Why does He bless us as He does?

The scripture says that "we're blessed to be a blessing."

That's why the King James Version says He will teach you to *profit* … which is also defined in Strong's Concordance as to *gain.*

6. I will show you what to do.

There are times in life when we think we know what we're doing without consulting God, and even more foolishly, we think we know what God wants by looking at things through our own reasoning.

Samuel was directed by God to anoint the next king of Israel. He was sent to Jesse's house where he thought he was looking at all of his sons.

God gave Samuel very specific instructions ... he told the prophet that He would tell him which son to anoint.

1 Samuel 16:3 in the New International Version says:

> *"Invite Jesse to the sacrifice, and I will show you what to do. You are to anoint for me the one I indicate."*

There are times in life when we're confident in what we're

thinking only to realize later that we really didn't have a clue.

1 Samuel 16:6 in the Amplified Bible says:

> *"When they had come, he looked on Eliab [the eldest son] and said, Surely the Lord's anointed is before Him."*

Eliab was not God's choice … neither were any of the other brothers who were present. **When Samuel asked the right question** ... are all your sons here ... God showed him what to do. Jesse had to send to the fields to bring David to the sacrifice.

When you follow His instructions … listen to His voice ... then He will show you what to do.

7. I will show you where to go.

Jeremiah 1:7 in the Message Bible says:

> *"God told me, 'Don't say, "I'm only a boy." I'll tell you where to go and you'll go there. I'll tell you what to say and you'll say it. Don't be afraid of a soul. I'll be right there, looking after you.' "*

God will not only show you where to go ... He will tell you what to say.

Obedience to His Word ... also brings freedom from fear in anything or anyone you may be facing ... because He will always be right there ... looking after you.

God makes an exceedingly wonderful promise in the last part of Hebrews 13:5. The Amplified Bible puts it this way:

> *"... for He [God] Himself has said, I will not in any way fail you nor give you up nor leave you without support. [I will] not, [I will] not, [I will] not in any degree leave you helpless nor forsake nor let [you] down (relax My hold on you)! [Assuredly not!]"*

Isaiah 48:17 brings out the richness of what God promises to us ... I love this scripture. How about you?

My friend Randy sent me a text this morning … that said … "To teach is to learn twice."

That's so true.

Day 5

7 Things To Do If You Want To Be Rich

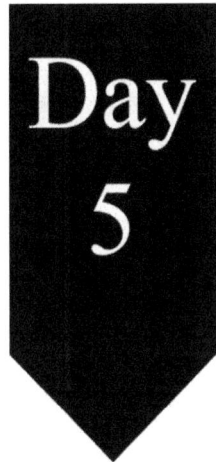

Do you want to be rich?

When people hear that question ... many think ... they're about to hear the latest pitch for a network marketing business, overseas investment opportunity or some get-rich quick scheme.

Actually, when I say you can be rich ... I'm not sharing what somebody else says ... or even what I think ... I'm giving you the principles found in the Word of God.

It's important to note ... there is a scriptural progression if you want to become rich.

Proverbs 10:22 tells us the formula for God's riches ... and who would want anything else?

The Amplified Bible says:

> *"The blessing of the Lord—it makes [truly] rich, and He [God] adds no sorrow with it [neither does toiling increase it]."*

Riches are the result of God's blessing on our lives.

Isaiah 1:16-17 in the Amplified Bible says:

> *"Wash yourselves, make yourselves clean; put away the evil of your doings from before My eyes! Cease to do evil, learn to do right! Seek justice, relieve the oppressed, and correct the oppressor. Defend the fatherless, plead for the widow."*

This scripture gives us seven things we are instructed to do.

1. Wash ourselves ... inside and out.

In searching the scriptures ... frequently people were told to wash their outer bodies and then their inner bodies ... mind and heart.

Jesus made this distinction in Matthew 23:26 when He says:

> *"You blind Pharisee! First clean the inside of the cup and of the plate, so that the outside may be clean also."*

When we're clean before Him ... we're ready for His use.

2 Timothy 2:21 in the New Living Translation says:

> *"If you keep yourself pure, you will be a special utensil for honorable use. Your life will be clean, and you will be ready for the Master to use you for every good work."*

2. Stop looking at evil.

When you look at something ... you're focusing on that person and/or object. The Word of God is clear that He doesn't want us looking at such things ... if we don't want to live below our spiritual pay grade.

1 John 2:16 in the Amplified Bible says:

> *"For all that is in the world– the lust of the flesh [craving for sensual gratification] and the lust of the eyes [greedy longings of the mind] and the pride of life [assurance in one's own resources or in the stability of earthly things]– these do not come from the Father but are from the world [itself]."*

Proverbs 15:3 says:

> *"The eyes of the LORD are in every place, beholding the evil and the good."*

3. Stop doing evil.

It's not enough to stop looking at evil ... those with evil ways must also stop. There is an immediate as well as an eternal benefit when a person stops doing evil.

Jeremiah 25:5 says:

> *"They said, Turn ye again now everyone from his evil way, and from the evil of your doings, and dwell in the land that the LORD hath given unto you and to your fathers for ever and ever."*

4. Learn to do right.

Regardless of our background, up-bringing or educational experience ... we all have to learn to do what is right in His sight ... but doing right is a conscious, individual choice.

Job 34:4 in the New International Reader's Version says:

> *"So let's choose for ourselves what is right. Let's learn together what is good."*

Proverbs 9:9 in the New Living Translation says:

> *"Instruct the wise, and they will be even wiser. Teach the righteous, and they will learn even more."*

5. Bring relief to those who are oppressed.

The reason God wants us to help the oppressed ... is because we are His agents on the earth.

Psalm 22:24 in the GOD'S WORD Translation says:

> *"The Lord has not despised or been disgusted with the plight of the oppressed one. He has not hidden his face from that person. The Lord heard when that oppressed person cried out to him for help."*

God hears the cry of the oppressed, and He's calling on us to do something about it.

Psalm 72:12 in the New Living Translation says:

"He will rescue the poor when they cry to him; he will help the oppressed, who have no one to defend them."

When we make ourselves available to help the oppressed, then blessings are coming our way.

Proverbs 14:31 in the New Living Translation says:

"Those who oppress the poor insult their Maker, but helping the poor honors him."

6. Care for the orphans.

I have written extensively about helping the widows and the orphans and how it pleases the Lord.

When it comes to caring for the orphans ... one scripture says it best.

James 1:27 in the Amplified Bible says:

"External religious worship [religion as it is expressed in outward acts] that is pure and unblemished in the sight of God the Father is this: to visit and help and care for the orphans and widows in their affliction and need, and to keep oneself unspotted and uncontaminated from the world."

7. Help the widows.

Every day I'm confronted with sad stories from widows

who are barely surviving … some because their late husband never did any financial planning or worse spent every dime they had.

I have also seen widows who've lost all they had helping children who take advantage of a mother's heart.

What are you and I to do about the widows … especially those in our own household? 1 Timothy 5:8 says:

> *"But if any provide not for his own, and specially for those of his own house, he hath denied the faith, and is worse than an infidel."*

The Contemporary English Version of James 1:27 says:

> *"Religion that pleases God the Father must be pure and spotless. You must help needy orphans and widows and not let this world make you evil."*

Luke 11:41 in the New Living Translation says:

> *"So clean the inside by giving gifts to the poor, and you will be clean all over."*

As you implement the instructions found in Isaiah 1:16-17 ... look at the promises found in Isaiah 1:18 in the Living Bible.

> *"Come, let's talk this over, says the Lord; no matter how deep the stain of your sins, I can take it out and make you as clean as freshly fallen snow. Even if you are stained as red as crimson, I can make*

> *you white as wool!"*

Put your spiritual seat belt on ... as you read Isaiah 1:19 from the Living Bible. It says:

> *"If you will only let me help you, if you will only obey, then I will make you rich!"*

Read Verse 19 one more time.

> *"If you will only let me help you, if you will only obey, then I will make you rich."*

Hallelujah!!

The key point of this teaching is how to become rich ... so it's important to fully understand that when the scripture says, *"If you will only let me help you, if you will only obey,"* it clearly means we have a choice.

When does God help us? The answer is simple: **when we listen to what He has to say and follow His instructions ... when we obey His Word.** However, if we fail to follow these seven instructions ... we will face a less then desirable response from the Lord.

When we follow God's instructions ... when we do the seven things He tells us to do … He will make us rich ... but the choice is ours.

4 Questions About the Next 300 Days

Two months is just over 60 days. In the last two months … we've been walking … planning … trying to achieve our goals … leaving us just over 300 days to change our destiny before we begin our year over again ... 300 days to do what we've never done ... become what we've never been ... be what God created and ordained us to be.

I was directed this wonderful morning to ask you four questions.

1. **Have you been making a list of the ways in which God has manifested His presence in your life every day?**

In a previous teaching ... I encouraged everyone to read "7 Things To Do Before You Go To Sleep."

The second thing you should do before going to sleep is "... journal the great things that happened to you during the day." Regardless of how your day went ... you have something to rejoice over. If nothing else, and I mean nothing else ... you have the ability to read the words I'm writing.

"I GUARANTEE … you'll sleep better at night if you end your day by praising God."

I recently had a very successful real estate investor in Florida tell me that doing the seven things from my teaching before going to sleep ... changed his life and the way he thinks.

Colossians 4:2 in the New International Version says:

> *"Devote yourselves to prayer, being watchful and thankful."*

We are to be watchful for opportunities and thankful when they come.

2. **The second question I want to ask you is ... how are you coming on your goals for this year?**

Did you write out your goals for this year?

If so, how are you coming in the six major areas of your life?

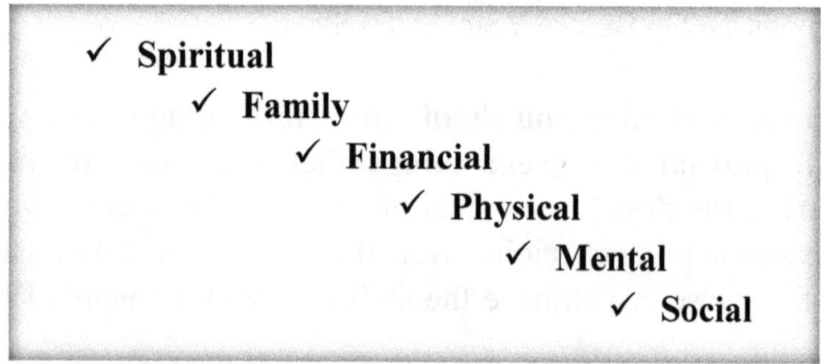

If you didn't write them out ... as my fine wife Bev says ... you haven't missed your opportunity … do it now.

Habakkuk 2:2-3 in the Message Bible says:

> *"And then God answered: 'Write this. Write what you see. Write it out in big block letters so that it can be read on the run. This vision-message is a witness pointing to what's coming. It aches for the coming—it can hardly wait! And it doesn't lie. If it seems slow in coming, wait. It's on its way. It will come right on time.' "*

Don't overthink this ... just let it flow. The number of goals you have isn't nearly as important as you having them.

3. **The third question is ... have you written the plans and created the timeline to accomplish the goals you set 60 days ago?**

The first thing you need to do before you go to sleep at night is ... create a "to do" list of the things you plan to accomplish tomorrow. List them by priorities based on your goals in the six major areas of your life ... spiritual, family, financial, physical, mental and social.

1 Timothy 4:15 in the New Living Translation says:

> *"Give your complete attention to these matters. Throw yourself into your tasks so that everyone will see your progress."*

I strongly encourage you to visit our website to read or re-read "7 Keys to Planning Your Work and Working Your Plan."

4. **Lastly, what steps are you taking to renew your mind on a daily basis for the rest of this year?**

After giving me these questions … the Lord directed me to Romans 12:2 in the Amplified Bible which says:

> *"Do not be conformed to this world (this age), [fashioned after and adapted to its external, superficial customs], but be transformed (changed) by the [entire] renewal of your mind [by its new ideals and its new attitude], so that you may prove [for yourselves] what is the good and acceptable and perfect will of God, even the thing which is good and acceptable and perfect [in His sight for you]."*

After reading this verse ... the Lord gave me a word to pass on to you.

> ***"Do not be conformed to this world (this age), [fashioned after and adapted to its external, superficial customs]."***

The Greek word for "conformed" means "to conform one's self (i.e. one's mind and character) to another's pattern."

Popular culture and advertisers are continually trying to mold you to their thought processes and value system. **They want you to think the way they think ... do the things they do ... buy the things they say to buy ... and live the way they say you should live.**

In popular terminology "they" want to clone you into a spender of your hard-earned money when, where and how they say you should. **They couldn't care less if you get in debt … that's not their problem.**

Their primary mission is to relieve you of your money ... the result of which will oftentimes prevent you from doing the very things that God says will bring you into an abundant life ... the kind that He promises and the kind that only He can give.

If you awaken in the morning to a clock radio morning show ... **the first sounds you hear every day are trying to mold you into the image of the ideal consumer** ... one who does what he or she is told when they're told to do it.

The unsuspecting consumer is bombarded with continual thoughts of what advertisers call The Good Life.

Make no mistake about it ... **the key to your future is in your thought life.**

Sow a Thought ... Reap an Action

The advertisers sow appealing and oftentimes seductive thoughts trying to convince you that the only way you can enjoy The Good Life is by buying their products.

They don't care if their actions throw you further into debt.

Sow an Action ... Reap a Habit

If we act on the marketing schemes of advertisers ... if we fall prey to their pitches, we will reap a habit of buying without considering the consequences of our actions.

Sow a Habit ... Reap Your Character

The type of thinking that allows us to buy things we can't afford with money we don't have simply to impress people who probably don't even like us is a habit we can't afford. It reflects character values that aren't scriptural.

Sow Your Character ... Reap Your Destiny

When we conform to an advertiser's way of thinking ... we ignore the Word of God and yield our future and destiny into someone else's control … often without even being aware of it.

That's not God's plan for us.

Truth Alert from the Word of God:

1 Peter 1:14 in the Amplified Bible says:

> *"[Live] as children of obedience [to God]; **do not conform yourselves to the evil desires [that governed you] in your former ignorance** [when you did not know the requirements of the Gospel]."*

The Message Bible says:

> *"Don't lazily slip back into those old grooves of evil, doing just what you feel like doing. You didn't know any better then; you do now. As obedient children, let yourselves be pulled into a way of life shaped by God's life, a life energetic and blazing with holiness."*

The only way we can live a life shaped by God's life, a life energetic and blazing with holiness, is by the renewal of our minds.

The only way we can change our destiny ... to fulfill God's perfect will for our lives … is to make a determined effort to get in His presence ... follow His Word ... take control of our thought processes ... think on and speak only those things that are for the spiritual progress and edification of ourselves and those around us.

The Lord wants us to think before we act ... He wants us transformed to His image ... thinking as He thinks ... doing what He would do with the dawn of each new day.

We have 300 days remaining to make this the greatest year of our lives ... our year of unfulfilled promises … FULFILLED.

Why not start today? Why not start right now?

Don't forget this wonderful scripture I've quoted before … 2 Corinthians 5:17 in the Amplified Bible which says:

> "*Behold, the fresh and new has come!*"

Are you ready? He wants you to be!

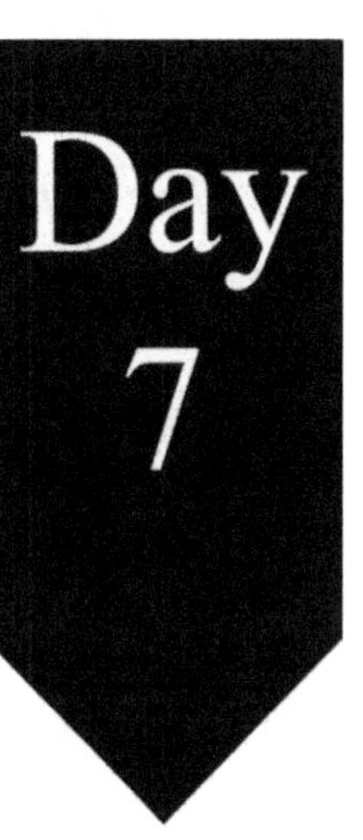

7 Seven "E's" for Strong Faith

Have you ever had someone tell you they will give you an "E" for effort?

What does that mean? Is that supposed to make you feel better? Look, if I expended the effort ... I know what I did.

Not meaning to sound ungrateful here but I never want to be recognized for just being in the game of life ... **I always want to cross the finish line first ... with my arms lifted up ... giving God all the praise, honor and glory for making it happen.**

When I strive for a goal ... my faith is always extended ... that's why I'm going to share with you seven keys or "E's" for strong faith.

I'm talking about mountain-moving, devil-chasing, debt-cancelling, wealth-building, bondage-breaking, yoke-destroying, assignment-making, life-changing and destiny-shaping faith.

1. **Expand your boundaries ... geographically and mentally.**

Do you believe that Acts 10:34 is the whole truth and

nothing but the truth?

> *"Then Peter opened his mouth, and said, Of a truth I perceive that God is no respecter of persons."*

Are you confident beyond a shadow of a doubt that your Heavenly Father is no respecter of persons ... that what He's done for one believer ... He will do for you?

I trust your answer would be an emphatic "YES." Truth be told ... anyone who doubts Acts 10:34 may well doubt other parts of the scriptures as well.

If you know God is no respecter of persons then you know He will do for you what He did for Jabez in 1 Chronicles 4:9-10 (New Living Translation). It says:

> *"There was a man named Jabez who was more honorable than any of his brothers. His mother named him Jabez because his birth had been so painful. He was the one who prayed to the God of Israel, 'Oh, that you would bless me and expand my territory! Please be with me in all that I do, and keep me from all trouble and pain!' And God granted him his request."*

God wants to expand your territory ... enlarge your borders ... move you from where you are to a total higher level of success in and through Him.

Yes, He wants to expand the boundaries of your sphere of influence, but He also wants to expand your mental capacity as well.

Psalm 119:32 in the New Living Translation says:

> *"I will pursue your commands, for you expand my understanding."*

If you haven't read *The Prayer of Jabez,* I encourage you to do so. Go to a website such as www.amazon.com or any Christian bookstore.

2. Elevate your conversation to a higher spiritual and success level.

Eliminate the words ... quit ... can't ... try ... failure ... negative ... compromise ... from your vocabulary.

Guard your heart ... for out of the abundance of it ... the mouth will speak.

Ephesians 4:29 in the Amplified Bible says:

> *"Let no foul or polluting language, nor evil word nor unwholesome or worthless talk [ever] come out of your mouth, but only such [speech] as is good and beneficial to the spiritual progress of others, as is fitting to the need and the occasion, that it may be a blessing and give grace (God's favor) to those who hear it."*

Speak the pure, the powerful and the positive from the Word of God over every person and situation that you deal with.

Take the time to write down something positive about the

people you deal with on a regular basis and let that become the focal point of your next conversation with them.

3. Expect divine appointments and supernatural connections every day ... starting TODAY.

As you pursue your goals ... raise your level of expectation for divine appointments and supernatural connections ... to people that God can use to get you from where you are to where He wants you to be.

God can bring the right person into your life ... just like that.

1 Samuel 9:15-16 in the Message Bible says:

> *"The very day before, God had confided in Samuel, '<u>This time tomorrow</u>, I'm sending a man from the land of Benjamin to meet you. You're to anoint him as prince over my people Israel. He will free my people from Philistine oppression. Yes, I know all about their hard circumstances. I've heard their cries for help.' "*

Saul was a donkey herder until he had a divine appointment. Be vigilant ... be watchful ... be expectant ... but never be judgmental about who or how God chooses to be ... your supernatural connection.

If you want to start a business, spend time with people who have expertise in your new field of endeavor. Ask their opinions ... seek their advice ... don't tell them your secrets ... but show yourself friendly.

4. **Endue yourself with a spiritual awareness of who you're working for and how that relates to your goal of career advancement and other income opportunities.**

What have you done today ... this week ... this month ... this year to increase your value as an employee to your current employer?

If your answer to that question in any way contains anything negative about your current employer, then you will never advance beyond where you are, because you have the wrong perspective.

First, you should get Colossians 3:17, 23 down in your spirit.

> *"And whatsoever ye do in word or deed, do all in the name of the Lord Jesus, giving thanks to God and the Father by him."*
>
> *"And whatsoever ye do, do it heartily, as to the Lord, and not unto men."*

Second, you must realize that everything you do on the job ... you are doing as unto the Lord. He's the one who will cover your employee evaluation.

Once you realize you're working for the Lord ... you will find a new desire for excellence in all your hands find to do ... on the job.

When you are faithful where you are ... then He will open other opportunities beyond your wildest dreams.

5. Enjoy the benefits of a good job.

Your attitude will turn an average job into an above average job.

Ecclesiastes 5:18 says:

> *"Behold that which I have seen: it is good and comely for one to eat and to drink, and to enjoy the good of all his labour that he taketh under the sun all the days of his life, which God giveth him: for it is his portion."*

God has a portion for you … can somebody say Hallelujah!!!

6. Establish family time that is written in stone.

Ecclesiastes 11:4 in the Living Bible says that if you wait for perfect conditions you'll never get anything done.

There should be some absolutes in your life ... first, your time with God is immoveable. Second, create real value and lasting memories with your family time.

When I come home for dinner ... my cell phone is placed on a table, and I rarely, if ever, answer it during dinner. When our daughters lived at home there was no texting during our meals. That may seem like a little thing ... but understand that each of them sent and/or received between 8,000 and 11,000 text messages a month.

When you're with your family ... be with your family.

7. Energize your faith.

How do you energize your faith? It's simple ... with the Word of God and time in His presence. That's it pure and simple ... however, I feel impressed to share three scriptures with you.

1 Corinthians 12:6 in the Amplified Bible says:

> *"And there are distinctive varieties of operation [of working to accomplish things], but it is the same God Who inspires and energizes them all in all."*

Ecclesiastes 7:12 in the Message Bible says:

> *"Double protection: wisdom and wealth! Plus this bonus: Wisdom energizes its owner."*

This list of powerful "E" words could go on ... I haven't even covered empower, enlighten, enable, extend and entertain ... just to name a few ... but it's time for me to END this teaching.

7 Keys To Thrive While Others Survive

The measure of a person's character is determined by how he or she handles success and adversity.

When everything we touch prospers ... we love to quote Deuteronomy 8:18:

> *"But thou shalt remember the LORD thy God: for it is he that giveth thee power to get wealth ..."*

When we and our loved ones walk free of sickness and disease ... we love to quote 3 John 2 in the Amplified Bible:

> *"Beloved, I pray that you may prosper in every way and [that your body] may keep well, even as [I know] your soul keeps well and prospers."*

When our bank, investment and retirement accounts are running over ... we love to quote 2 Corinthians 9:8 in the Amplified Bible:

> *"And God is able to make all grace (every favor and earthly blessing) come to you in abundance, so that you may always and under all circumstances and whatever the need be self-sufficient [possessing enough to require no aid or*

support and furnished in abundance for every good work and charitable donation]."

When we have a house, a condo at the beach and/or rental properties ... we love to quote Mark 10:30 in the Amplified Bible:

"Who will not receive a hundred times as much now in this time—houses and brothers and sisters and mothers and children and lands, with persecutions—and in the age to come, eternal life."

I could go on ... because the precious promises of God are so numerous. When someone walks in the kind of blessing flow that I've just described ... it's easy to Praise God for His many manifold blessings.

When things are good ... it's easy to praise God ... but what happens when things aren't so good?

There are so many similarities between the times of Habakkuk and the 21st century in which we live.

In Habakkuk's time ... immorality, greed, and injustice were prevalent.

The line between right and wrong was so blurred that people who said they believed in God were doing wrong things thinking it was all right. The prevailing thought in the society was ... "If it feels good ... do it ... again."

It's never right to do a wrong thing to create a right result.

Situational ethics compromise the Word of God.

God is long-suffering with us ... but Judgment Day is coming to a nation that turns its face and heart from our great God Jehovah.

The prophet saw a time coming when devastation would hit the land of Judah ... when God would use the evil Babylonians to punish His chosen people. The prophet foresaw a time when the vines, trees and ground would produce no fruit or vegetables to pick ... when there would be no livestock to tend ... there would be no jobs ... homes would be foreclosed on and there would be great suffering on the righteous and wicked alike.

Habakkuk 3:17-19 in the Message Bible says:

> *"Though the cherry trees don't blossom and the strawberries don't ripen, though the apples are worm-eaten and the wheat fields stunted, though the sheep pens are sheepless and the cattle barns empty, I'm singing joyful praise to God. I'm turning cartwheels of joy to my Savior God. Counting on God's Rule to prevail, I take heart and gain strength. I run like a deer. I feel like I'm king of the mountain!"*

The true measure of a person's spiritual depth and character is determined by his or her response to adversity.

Here are several questions ... that must be asked and answered.

Are God's promises true?

Are God's promises for you?

Are God's promises to you ... any less accurate because they have or have not as yet manifested in your life?

Absolutely not! **God's precious promises aren't based on current events, situational ethics or your present financial position.** His promises to you are conditional on but one thing ... your obedience to His instructions.

<u>God's Word is true regardless of what you're going through</u>. It is a manual to help us thrive while others just try to survive.

Will our obedience keep adversity away from our doorstep? No, but we can choose to keep the creator of trouble and adversity out of our mental and spiritual houses.

Here are <u>seven keys to thrive while others survive</u>.

1. **Allow God to bring peace to you in the midst of life's storms.**

When the storms of life are swirling around you, your family or your finances ... you have to do as Jesus did ... you must speak to your circumstances.

Mark 4:39-40 in the Amplified Bible says:

> *"And He arose and rebuked the wind and said to the sea, Hush now! Be still (muzzled)! And the wind ceased (sank to rest as if exhausted by its beating)*

and there was [immediately] a great calm (a perfect peacefulness). He said to them, Why are you so timid and fearful? How is it that you have no faith (no firmly relying trust)?"

Write your circumstances out ... speak the word over them ... and you will feel a peace that passes all understanding.

2. No weapon of any kind ... financial or otherwise ... can harm you.

Take comfort in the words and promises in the first part of Isaiah 54:17 in the Amplified Bible which says:

"But no weapon that is formed against you shall prosper, and every tongue that shall rise against you in judgment you shall show to be in the wrong ..."

What does *no* mean? None, Nada, nothing.

3. Your heritage assures your victory.

The remainder of Isaiah 54:17 in the Amplified Bible says:

"... This [peace, righteousness, security, triumph over opposition] is the heritage of the servants of the Lord [those in whom the ideal Servant of the Lord is reproduced]; this is the righteousness or the vindication which they obtain from Me [this is that which I impart to them as their justification], says the Lord."

The Hebrew word for heritage is more properly translated *inheritance*. No weapon formed against you prospering ... is your heritage as a born-again Child of God.

4. Your needs are known in heaven.

Matthew 6:8 says:

> *"Be not ye therefore like unto them: for your Father knoweth what things ye have need of, before ye ask him."*

5. You have a hedge of protection around you.

Acts 20:32 in the Amplified Bible says:

> *"And now [brethren], I commit you to God [I deposit you in His charge, entrusting you to His protection and care]. And I commend you to the Word of His grace [to the commands and counsels and promises of His unmerited favor]. It is able to build you up and to give you [your rightful] inheritance among all God's set-apart ones (those consecrated, purified, and transformed of soul)."*

6. Your deliverance from bondage is coming.

Exodus 14:13 in the Message Bible says:

> *"Moses spoke to the people: 'Don't be afraid. Stand firm and watch God do his work of salvation*

for you today. Take a good look at the Egyptians today for you're never going to see them again.' "

7. Not only is the Lord with you ... but He will never fail you.

2 Chronicles 20:17 in the New International Version says:

"You will not have to fight this battle. Take up your positions; stand firm and see the deliverance the LORD will give you, Judah and Jerusalem. Do not be afraid; do not be discouraged. Go out to face them tomorrow, and the LORD will be with you."

Deuteronomy 31:6 in the New Living Translation says:

"So be strong and courageous! Do not be afraid and do not panic before them. For the Lord your God will personally go ahead of you. He will neither fail you nor abandon you."

As you face adversity ... just remember the words of Psalm 3:8 in the Message Bible which says:

"Real help comes from God ..."

All the promises of the Lord are Yes and Amen!

Remember, whatever else you do:

1. Don't Forget Who Your Father Is.

2. Become His Best Student.

3. Master His Words.

4. Make Strategic Alliances with Fellow Students.
5. Have a Success and Victory.
6. Discipline Your Disappointments.
7. Focus on the Finish Line.

God bless … and have a day in the Lord filled with … victory!

7 Great Things To Do This Weekend

What are you doing this weekend?

Do you have a plan for your time?

Does it include ...

Shopping, social events, surfing the net, straightening up around the house, sports on TV, starting a home improvement project or shoveling snow or dirt in a flower bed ...

Or for some of us … relaxing around the pool or in front of a warm fire …

May I suggest that if you want to make next week ... your best week ever ... here are seven different things you should do this weekend … each one starting with the letter "R."

1. Rest

Some people find it hard to rest ... for a day ... let alone a weekend, due to what they perceive to be the demands of their jobs or perhaps the financial stress they're facing.

No matter what battles you're facing, take comfort in the words of Exodus 14:14 in the Amplified Bible:

> *"The Lord will fight for you, and you shall hold your peace and remain at rest."*

The Contemporary English Version of Exodus 14:14 says:

> *"The LORD will fight for you, and you won't have to do a thing."*

When you know that the Lord is fighting your battles ... that should release you to follow His instructions and rest.

The New Living Translation says that we're to "... *just stay calm.*"

There's a lot more that could be written about "rest" as it appears over 380 times in the King James Version of the Bible, but this is the verse God directed me to.

The bottom line is this ... we should find our rest in Him ... in His presence and His protection.

2. Relax

I just love the Lord ... He led me to three verses ... to help us understand the importance of relaxing.

In His Presence is a place where we can "relax" no matter what's going on around us.

Psalm 9:9 in the Message Bible says:

> *"God's a safe-house for the battered, a sanctuary during bad times. The moment you arrive, you relax; you're never sorry you knocked."*

We need to open our hearts to receive what God is sending our way.

Jude 1:1 in the Message Bible says:

> *"... Relax, everything's going to be all right; rest, everything's coming together; open your hearts, love is on the way!"*

When we allow ourselves to rest and relax in Him ... something good is coming our way.

Daniel 12:13 in the Message Bible says:

> *"And you? Go about your business without fretting or worrying. Relax. When it's all over, you will be on your feet to receive your reward."*

Can somebody say HALLELUJAH!!

3. Reflect

Psalm 119:15 in the New Living Translation says:

> *"I will study your commandments and reflect on your ways."*

I know God gave me a definite progression to these seven things. Rest, relax and now reflect. As we've been able to unwind in His presence, He is now going to give us some very specific instructions found in Titus 2:1, 7 in the New Living Translation which says:

> *"As for you, Titus, promote the kind of living that reflects wholesome teaching ... you yourself must be an example to them by doing good works of every kind. Let everything you do reflect the integrity and seriousness of your teaching."*

Make no mistake about it ... this scripture isn't just for Titus ... it's for each of us.

4. Refresh

Have you ever been really thirsty … where you could feel the first swallow of cool water going down your throat and into your stomach? Aahhh!

Do you remember how refreshing that drink of water was? But after a while ... you needed refreshing again.

Matthew 11:28 in the Amplified Bible offers us a "refreshing" that never ends.

> *"Come to Me, all you who labor and are heavy-laden and overburdened, and I will cause you to rest. [I will ease and relieve and refresh your souls.]"*

Did you notice the verse said "relieve" ... notice the

progression ... relieve and refresh.

Psalm 23:3 in the Amplified Bible says:

> *"He refreshes and restores my life (my self); He leads me in the paths of righteousness [uprightness and right standing with Him—not for my earning it, but] for His name's sake."*

5. Recreate

As the Lord stirred the word recreate in me … I thought surely He meant recreation.

You've rested the mind and the spirit … and that number five would be time to recreate as in recreation.

But after searching unsuccessfully for the word in 12 different translations ... I finally understood what He wanted me to share when I read Ephesians 2:10 in the Amplified Bible:

> *"For we are God's [own] handiwork (His workmanship), recreated in Christ Jesus, [born anew] that we may do those good works which God predestined (planned beforehand) for us [taking paths which He prepared ahead of time], that we should walk in them [living the good life which He prearranged and made ready for us to live]."*

If we're so weary that we can't think straight ... then we've limited our effectiveness to be able to do what He planned for us today.

God wants us resting, relaxing, reflecting and experiencing refreshing in His Presence so He can remind us that we are "... recreated in Christ Jesus ..." for a distinct purpose.

6. Reinvigorate

I realize that the word "reinvigorate" isn't in the scriptures ... it could have been the word "renewed." There are some pretty powerful scriptures that contain that word such as Psalm 94:19 in the New Living Translation:

> *"When doubts filled my mind, your comfort gave me renewed hope and cheer."*

Or 2 Corinthians 4:16 in the New Living Translation which says:

> *"That is why we never give up. Though our bodies are dying, our spirits are being renewed every day."*

Why reinvigorate? It's the word of choice because it symbolizes the fire of God that lives in your bones.

According to dictionary.com, it is defined as:

"to give vigor to; fill with life and energy; energize."

That's what I'm talking about. That is our passion for God's Word and our work.

7. Rejoice

Psalm 118:24 says:

> *"This is the day which the LORD hath made; we will rejoice and be glad in it."*

1 Thessalonians 5:16 in the Amplified Bible says:

> *"Be happy [in your faith] and rejoice and be glad-hearted continually (always)."*

I think the Message Bible translation of 1 Thessalonians 5:16-18 is a good scripture to end this teaching.

> *"Be cheerful no matter what; pray all the time; thank God no matter what happens. This is the way God wants you who belong to Christ Jesus to live."*

Seven practical things to do during your upcoming weekend ...

1. Read a book …

2. Write a book … spend an hour a day writing it … if you do that for 21 days ... something amazing will happen, and your book will become a reality.

3. Go for a walk … if it's still too cold ... walk inside the mall, but keep your wallet in your pocket. You're there to exercise your body ... not your credit cards.

4. Do something out of the ordinary. Make memories with your children. We love playing board games

… Monopoly … Balderdash … Banana Grams … choose a favorite of yours for your family.

5. Make a date with your spouse. My fine wife, Bev, was on the phone with me this morning ... we have grocery store dates ... laundry dates ... Wal-Mart dates ... and yes, movie dates during the afternoon when prices are cheaper (or we go to the dollar theater).

6. Get the family involved in finishing a project. Make a special dessert as a reward for their efforts.

7. Spend time talking about the Sunday sermon at church ... ask the kids what they learned in children's church ... talk about how to activate into daily life what they learned from the Word of God.

So what are you doing this weekend?

Let's see **… Rest … Relax … Reflect … Refresh … Recreate … Reinvigorate … and … Rejoice …**

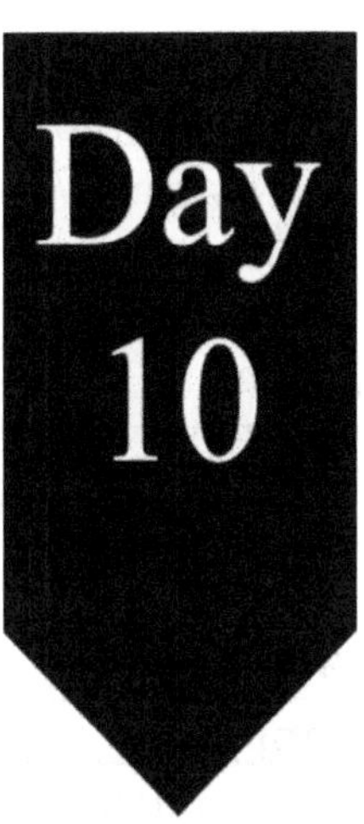

7 Ways To Find the Good in Bad Situations

Here are seven ways to look for the good in every bad situation … or how to overlook and overcome the mess we've made.

1. **First, YOU choose your outlook.**

Your inward disposition will always determine your outward outlook. That is why you must be grounded in God's Word. **<u>We cannot let what's happening around us affect what's living in us</u>.**

I'm going to say that again, because I want to make sure you got what I just said … it is a life-changing Rich Thought.

<u>We cannot let what's happening around us affect what's living in us</u>.

Regardless of the adversity ... no matter how messy or seemingly hopeless our situation may be ... our answer lies in our outlook.

Colossians 3:1-2 in the Message Bible says:

> *"[He Is Your Life] So if you're serious about living this new resurrection life with Christ,* ***<u>act like it</u>.***

Pursue the things over which Christ presides. Don't shuffle along, eyes to the ground, absorbed with the things right in front of you. Look up, and be alert to what is going on around Christ—that's where the action is. ***See things from his perspective.****"*

When we see things from His perspective ... we endure everything for the joy that is set before us.

Our outlook ... **our perspective on everything we're facing should never be subject to or formed by what's happening around us** ... but rather what's happening in and through us.

2. **Second, don't let anybody else's situation affect your outlook.**

My circle of friends "used to" include people who liked to commiserate ... people who wanted to hash and rehash the mess they were in. But my circle of friends doesn't include those kinds of folks any more.

Toxic talk and attitudes are contagious and infectious.

If you've been laid off from your job ... don't hang out with other folks who've been laid off as well. It's too easy to begin commiserating about how unfairly you were treated.

It's too easy to rehearse your hurts ... relive your frustration or anger ... talking yourself into thinking things are worse than they are. It's wasted energy that needs to be put toward making things better.

The dominant thoughts in our lives will draw similar

thoughts to them like a strong magnet.

3. Third, how do you get through the mess you've made?

Here are four things you need to get through it.

#1. You must acknowledge that you've messed up.

If you're alive on planet earth ... you've messed up. For some it's more of a habit than others, but no one's exempt.

#2. You need to stop living in denial.

You cannot live in DENIAL. Here's a fitting acronym for DENIAL.

Don't
Even
K**N**ow
I
Am
Lying (to myself)

#3. You need to leave the past behind.

If you've been forgiven ... you're just that ... forgiven ... so it's time to get up ... stop looking back.

#4. You need to move on.

Exodus 14:15 in the Living Bible says:

> *"Then the Lord said to Moses, 'Quit praying and get the people moving! Forward, march!' "*

4. Fourth, you have to stop dwelling on the bad situations you've faced.

There are times in our lives when we need to let something or someone go ... to move on.

This can be a rough process if you care for someone who doesn't care for you or someone you care about has hurt you deeply. But the truth of the matter is this, and I've said it many times before:

You cannot control what other people do, but you can control what you do.

We must get over certain situations ... adversaries who want to hold us back from fulfilling God's destiny for our lives. Our trust must be in Him and His Word.

Psalm 119:133 in the New Living Translation says:

> *"Guide my steps by your word, so I will not be overcome by evil."*

Proverbs 4:23-27 in the Message Bible says:

> *"Keep vigilant watch over your heart; that's where life starts. Don't talk out of both sides of your mouth; avoid careless banter, white lies, and gossip. Keep your eyes straight ahead; ignore all sideshow distractions.* ***Watch your step****, and the road will stretch out smooth before you. Look neither right nor left; leave evil in the dust."*

How do you watch over your heart? It's simply by what you put in your mind or you allow your mind to focus on.

For out of the abundance of the heart ... the mouth speaks.

5. **Fifth, you have to give yourself a spiritual pep talk.**

Did you ever attend a pep rally in high school or college ... where the sole purpose of the cheerleaders or pep squad was to motivate your team spirit?

The number one purpose of a pep rally is to get you involved even though you'll be sitting in the bleachers during the big game.

In the big event ... you're not sitting in the bleachers or standing on the sidelines, my friend. You are the game ... and you need to be your most important cheerleader or pep squad team member.

In the game of life there will be times when there's no one around except ... you and the Lord. As a result **you must become your greatest fan ... your own pep squad leader.** It will be your responsibility to encourage yourself ... but you will have help.

First, Deuteronomy 3:28 says:

> *"But charge Joshua, and encourage him, and strengthen him: for he shall go over before this people, and he shall cause them to inherit the land which thou shalt see."*

If allowed, the Holy Spirit will strengthen, encourage and motivate you to even greater levels of accomplishment. But in the final analysis ... you must be responsible for your own encouragement.

Second, 1 Samuel 30:6 in the Amplified Bible says:

> *"David was greatly distressed, for the men spoke of stoning him because the souls of them all were bitterly grieved, each man for his sons and daughters. But David encouraged and strengthened himself in the Lord his God."*

How do you encourage or give yourself a spiritual pep talk? It's easy. **Use the Word of God to motivate yourself from where you are ... to where God wants you to be.**

6. **Sixth, you gotta roll up your sleeves and do whatever is necessary.**

Some people wonder why they're never promoted on the job ... it's because they just do what's required ... never taking the extra step that is going to put them above the crowd.

If you want to succeed in life ... you must always do more than is required.

Titus 3:14 in the Amplified Bible says:

> *"And let our own [people really] learn to apply themselves to good deeds (to honest labor and honorable employment), so that they may be able to meet necessary demands whenever the occasion may require and not be living idle and uncultivated and unfruitful lives."*

God wants you to be fruitful ... to do more than is required. He wants you to go the extra mile ... that's the only way you'll ever overcome every bad situation you face.

7. **Seventh, looking through bad situations will bring you an even greater reward.**

When you show yourself faithful ... when you do not grow weary in well-doing ... when you overcome bad situations ... when you endure the mess of life ... then God will lift you up and set your inheritance before you.

Galatians 6:9 in the Amplified Bible says:

> *"And let us not lose heart and grow weary and faint in acting nobly and doing right, for in due time and at the appointed season we shall reap, if we do not loosen and relax our courage and faint."*

The New Living Translation says we shall *"... reap a harvest of blessings, if we don't give up."*

Remember, when we endure bad situations ... God will lift us up and set our inheritance before us.

Day 11

7 Essential "P" Ingredients for Success

Every time I think I've read and/or written everything I could possibly write about success … God shows me something else.

I was reading a book ... frankly, I don't even remember which one … when I felt prompted to write down the seven essential ingredients of success.

I picked up my iPad and immediately wrote:

Purpose, passion, preparation, plan, persistence, power and promotion.

When I noticed all the essential ingredients of success started with the letter "P" … I thought for a moment that I was on a spiritual Sesame Street.

1. **The first essential ingredient to success is purpose.**

Dictionary.com defines purpose as:

a. **the reason for which something exists or is done, made, used, etc.**

b. **an intended or desired result; end; aim; goal.**

God Has A Purpose For Your Life.

Say it out loud: **GOD HAS A PURPOSE FOR MY LIFE** … now personalize and write it down.

Without your purpose identified firmly in your mind, you will wander through life, never quite feeling that you're "in the flow."

And let me be clear, your PURPOSE may have nothing to do with how you make money (your job) … because you can make MONEY in many ways that **may not be directly related to your purpose** … although you can still glorify God while doing your job.

Purpose gives meaning to WHY you're doing what you're doing.

It's time to listen to that inner voice, to **give serious attention to what comes naturally to you … to what gets YOU juiced,** and I don't mean steroids … to what gets YOU moving at the start of each day ... and each new week.

When you have the **right purpose**, you'll more easily **develop the right vision.** When you have the **right vision**, you'll quickly **recognize the right goal.**

Always remember what Proverbs 19:21 in the New Living Translation says:

> *"You can make many plans, but the Lord's purpose will prevail."*

2. **The second essential ingredient to success is**

passion.

As I thought about passion I wrote the following acronym:

Positive
Attitude
Supernatural
Surge
Intensity
Overwhelming
Negativity

A person with passion has a "**P**ositive **A**ttitude causing a **S**upernatural **S**urge in **I**ntensity **O**verwhelming all **N**egativity."

Passion or the lack of it ... is contagious.

Your passion for life and success ... needs to spread to others ... it needs to go viral in order to illuminate your personal commitment ... your passion to succeed.

Your passion will also determine your spiritual attire.

Listen to Isaiah 59:17 in the New International Version which says:

> *"He put on righteousness as his body armor and placed the helmet of salvation on his head. He clothed himself with a robe of vengeance and wrapped himself in a cloak of divine passion."*

3. **The third essential ingredient to success is preparation.**

After purpose and passion ... there must be preparation.

The World English Dictionary defines preparation as:

"the act or process of preparing and the state of being prepared; readiness."

Preparation for action is a mental decision before it manifests as a practical reality.

Psalm 90:12 says:

> *"So teach us to number our days, that we may apply our hearts unto wisdom."*

I've shared before the meaning of the word *number* but it bears repeating. The Hebrew word for *number* is **manah** (H4487) in the Strong's Concordance and it means:

"to count, reckon, assign, tell, appoint, prepare."

I think it's significant that the definition of number includes the words "assign," "appoint" and "prepare."

That last one is where we get the word **preparation.**

It's clear that "to number our days" means more than just counting them on a calendar.

We're to assign our days.

Have you read, and are you implementing the wisdom in the teaching "7 Things To Do Before You Go To Sleep"? If so, you know that before you pillow your head at night ... you're to appoint your days ... give each day a special purpose. Don't just allow it to happen without your involvement in what's happening in it.

We're to prepare our days.

4. **The fourth essential ingredient to success is planning.**

Planning takes your purpose, passion and mental preparation ... and brings them into a plan of action.

What's your plan for each new day?

Is your plan to let things happen or to make things happen?

Only you can control your day.

Psalm 90:12 in the Contemporary English Version says:

> *"Teach us to use wisely all the time we have."*

With prior proper planning you will insure your success.

Proverbs 21:5 in the New International Version says:

> *"The plans of the diligent lead to profit as surely as haste leads to poverty."*

1 Timothy 4:15 in the New Living Translation says:

> *"Give your complete attention to these matters. Throw yourself into your tasks so that everyone will see your progress."*

5. **The fifth essential ingredient to success is persistence.**

What does the Word of God say about persistence?

Revelation 2:2 in the Message Bible says:

> *"I see what you've done, your hard, hard work, your refusal to quit. I know you can't stomach evil, that you weed out apostolic pretenders. I know your persistence, your courage in my cause that you never wear out."*

This is such a powerful verse.

Persistence is one of the main keys to success in life.

Dale Carnegie, the author of *How to Win Friends and Influence People,* said:

"Flaming enthusiasm, backed up by horse sense and persistence, is the quality that most frequently makes for success."

President Calvin Coolidge said:

"Nothing in this world can take the place of persistence. Talent will not; nothing is more common than unsuccessful people with talent. Genius will not; unrewarded genius is almost a proverb."

6. **The sixth essential ingredient to success is power.**

There are some things I say ... that bear repeating. Several weeks back ... I spoke a five-word sentence that should be repeated over and over again until it gets deep inside of us. Here it is:

"<u>God hasn't left us powerless</u>."

Acts 1:8 says:

> *"... ye shall receive power, after that the Holy Ghost is come upon you ... (then) ye shall become witnesses ..."*

The power Jesus promises after the Holy Ghost comes upon you is enabling power.

The Greek word **dunamis** has three primary meanings:

"strength, power, ability."

So let's look at Acts 1:8 again as I expand the paraphrase for you.

> *"You shall receive the ability after the Holy Ghost has come upon you, and you will be able to witness of me simultaneously in Jerusalem, and in Judea, and in Samaria, and to the uttermost parts of the earth."*

What kind of witness should you be for Him? We can gain a fresh insight by looking at the other definitions of the word dunamis also:

"power for performing miracles; moral power and excellence of soul; the power and influence which belong to riches and wealth."

You shall receive the power for performing miracles ... you shall receive the power of moral excellence and you shall receive the power of influence with riches and wealth.

7. The seventh essential ingredient to success is promotion.

Have you ever been promoted?

From one grade to the next in school ... from one level of accomplishment to the next in the Boy or Girl Scouts ... from one rank to a higher one in the military or from one position to a different one at your place of employment? Or from owning one store to opening another?

If you think the promotion was a result of your skills and/or your hard work, then I suggest you read, study and meditate on Psalm 75:6-8 in the Living Bible:

> *"For promotion and power come from nowhere on earth, but only from God. He promotes one and deposes another."*

Your promotion comes from the Lord. He gives you the power and favor for advancement in every single area of human endeavor.

I've shared with you seven essential P's for success ... I realize that I left out the most obvious one ... prayer. But truthfully, if you're not praying ... then none of the rest of this teaching will be of real and lasting value to you.

I encourage you to reread this teaching several times ... maybe even take out a pencil and make your own personal notes and "to do" list in the margin.

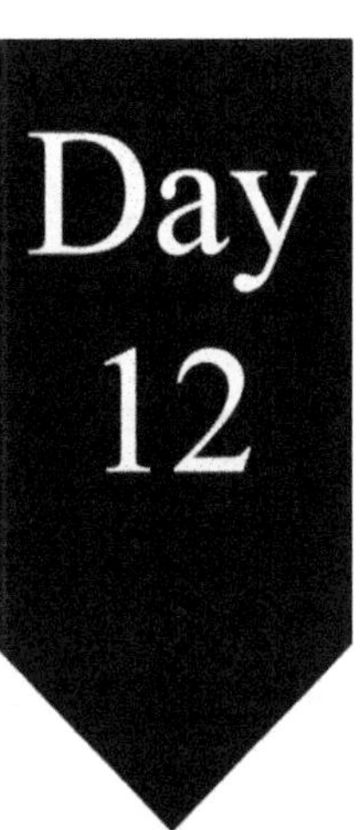

7 Keys To Taking a Step of Faith

Here's the question of the day:

How do WE move from where we are … to manifesting the blessing of God in our lives?

Here's the bottom line … we've got to take a step of faith.

Psalm 37:23 says:

> *"The steps of a good man are ordered by the LORD: and He delighteth in his way."*

Personalize that scripture …

> *"The steps of [Name] are ordered by the LORD: and [he/she] delighteth in his way."*

A walk of faith … is a series of steps …

When you take a step of faith it releases the power of God in and through your life.

Here are the seven keys to taking a step of faith:

1. **A step of faith is a decision.**

It is a decision … a commitment to pursue a promise without a visual of the desired result in sight.

Dr. Martin Luther King Jr. said:

"Take the first step in faith. You don't have to see the whole staircase, just take the first step."

A walk of faith is a series of decisions we make on a daily basis.

God calls on people to take a step of faith so that miracles will be made manifest in their lives.

Can somebody say ... Hallelujah!!

2. A step of faith requires action on our part.

When Jesus said he would heal someone … he often used the Greek word **ther-a-pay** from which we get the word therapy.

Jesus would "therapy" them or require them to participate themselves … like "reach out your hand" or "go wash in the pool."

In the same way, **many scriptures require that we first do something before we receive the promise of God**.

Jesus tells the nobleman with a dying child to go his way … the man believed and went home to see his child healed …

Do we have that kind of faith? What if Benny Hinn with his healing anointing spoke that word into our lives?

John 4:49-51 says:

> *"The nobleman saith unto him, Sir, come down ere my child die. Jesus saith unto him, Go thy way; thy son liveth. And* ***the man believed the word that Jesus had spoken unto him, and he went his way.*** *And as he was now going down, his servants met him, and told him, saying, Thy son liveth."*

3. A step of faith requires obedience.

Jesus tells the ten lepers to go show the priest that they were healed … but it wasn't until the lepers began walking to the temple that they were healed.

Luke 17:14 says:

> *"And when he saw them, he said unto them, Go shew yourselves unto the priests. And it came to pass, that, as they went, they were cleansed."*

"… as they went …" **The miracle took place as they took a step of faith.**

Let me say it again … when they took a step of faith their miracle took place.

4. A step of faith requires you to look beyond your circumstances.

In Matthew 9:6 Jesus tells the paralyzed man lying on his bed to take a step of faith, and he began to walk.

> *"But that ye may know that the Son of man hath power on earth to forgive sins, (then saith he to the sick of the palsy,) Arise, take up thy bed, and go unto thine house."*

In Matthew 12:13 Jesus told the man with the withered hand in the synagogue to step forward and stretch it out.

> *"Then saith he to the man, Stretch forth thine hand. And he stretched it forth; and it was restored whole, like as the other."*

In Joshua 3:15-16 we read where Joshua took a step of faith by walking into the River Jordan … he took the step and the water stopped flowing … and the Israelites crossed … they took Jericho and the land of Canaan.

5. **A step of faith requires you to look for results in ways different than you expected.**

At the gate called Beautiful, Peter and John commanded the lame man to stand up and walk … to take a step of faith.

Acts 3:5 says:

> *"And he gave heed unto them, expecting to receive something of them."*

Acts 3:6 says:

> *"Then Peter said, Silver and gold have I none; but such as I have give I thee: In the name of Jesus Christ of Nazareth rise up and walk."*

The man was expecting someone to put food on his table for a day ... but what he received was a new lease on life.

Jesus called on Peter to step out of the boat and walk on the water …

Jesus gave him the authority, but nothing happened until Peter took a step of faith and got out of the boat.

Matthew 14:28-29 says:

> *"And Peter answered him and said, Lord, if it be thou, bid me come unto thee on the water. And he said, Come. And when Peter was come down out of the ship, he walked on the water, to go to Jesus."*

This occurred on the 4th watch, or roughly 3 AM in the morning, as it was nearing sunrise … they'd been struggling with the storm all night and yet were only halfway across.

Sometimes we will be required to take a step of faith in the midst of great adversity.

6. A step of faith may require a sacrifice.

The greatest step of faith in the scriptures was also a step of sacrifice … a very deep and personal sacrifice …

Abraham's readiness to give up his beloved son Isaac as an offering to God was both.

Abraham was prepared to carry out God's instructions even though he had waited one hundred years for this son; but now God wanted to know that Abraham was holding nothing back from Him.

Abraham displayed his faith even before he took his step of faith as he told his servants that he and the boy would return from sacrificing on the mountain.

Genesis 22:5 in the New Living Translation says:

> *" 'Stay here with the donkey,' Abraham told the young men. 'The boy and I will travel a little farther. We will worship there, and then we will come right back.' "*

Abraham did not offer one of his servants' children or even Ishmael because He knew that God was faithful to fulfill His promise.

Let's look at Hebrews 11:17-19 in the Amplified Bible which says:

> *"By faith Abraham, when he was put to the test [while the testing of his faith was still in progress], had already brought Isaac for an offering; he who had gladly received and welcomed [God's] promises was ready to sacrifice his only son, Of*

whom it was said, Through Isaac shall your descendants be reckoned. For he reasoned that God was able to raise [him] up even from among the dead. Indeed in the sense that Isaac was figuratively dead [potentially sacrificed], he did [actually] receive him back from the dead."

That's what God wants you to know ... that He's faithful to fulfill His promise.

7. A step of faith in sowing a seed leads to a great harvest.

The enemy of our future ... of our success ... of our victory does not want God's children walking by faith ... he does not want us moving in seed time and harvest.

The enemy understands the benefits and blessings for the believer who takes a step of faith by sowing a spirit-directed significant seed.

<u>The enemy hates offerings ... not just because they will ultimately cause the people of God to prosper, but because they contain spiritual power</u>.

The enemy hates it when you take a step of faith ... because he knows you are wise to his tricks, traps, lies and deceptions ... and yes, He knows you are on the way to victory.

Day 13

7 Reasons Not To Compare Yourself to Others

"Stop It."

When I heard those two words I was standing in a Half Price Books bookstore glancing through a book I was about to purchase. I looked around to see if one of the other customers had spoken those words to me ... they had not ... there was no one near me.

I knew the spirit of the Lord was clearly speaking to me, so I sat down at a table as I paused to hear His voice ... He said to me:

"Tell my children to stop comparing themselves to others. My Word and their obedience to it ... is the only measure of comparison my children should be concerned about."

I meditated on those words. **"Tell my children to stop comparing themselves to others."**

I realized that many people get themselves into financial trouble because they're always comparing themselves to others and the things they have or don't have.

I saw a recent survey that revealed that **the average age**

children get a cell phone is eight years old. Can you believe that?

Have your children or grandchildren ever asked you for a cell phone like "so and so" has? Every new cell phone release ... with the latest gadgets and widgets … prompts requests for a new phone.

By the way, it's not just the children that want the latest and greatest. It's moms and dads as well. Why do we have this "got to have it" attitude? It's simple … it comes from comparing what we have with what others have.

As I reflected on the Lord's words to me ... I felt stirred in my heart to write "7 Reasons Not To Compare Ourselves to Others."

1. **Inspect yourself.**

Galatians 6:4-5 in the GOD'S WORD Translation says:

> *"Each of you must examine your own actions. Then you can be proud of your own accomplishments without comparing yourself to others. Assume your own responsibility."*

We are accountable for our actions ... what we do or don't do.

There's more to it, though … how we act and react … what we say and don't say.

We can't blame anybody else for our actions. **We're the master of our own ship ... the creator of our own destiny** ... and we're to continually inspect what we're doing and compare how it lines up with His Word.

When we know that we've done the best job possible ... there is no need to compare ourselves to anybody else.

Galatians 6:4 in the New Living Translation says:

> *"Pay careful attention to your own work, for then you will get the satisfaction of a job well done, and you won't need to compare yourself to anyone else."*

2. Be proud but not prideful.

Let me simply suggest that being prideful is not a smart thing. Any doubts?

Deuteronomy 8:2 in the New Century Version says:

> *"Remember how the Lord your God has led you in the desert for these forty years, taking away your pride and testing you, because he wanted to know what was in your heart. He wanted to know if you would obey his commands."*

Child of God, it's much better that we deal with our pride ... instead of God dealing with it.

By the way, you can be proud of what you've accomplished ... as long as you recall and remember where your personal victories come from ... or more specifically, who they come from.

3. Don't compare yourself to others.

According to the scripture ... it's stupid to compare

ourselves to anyone else.

2 Corinthians 10:12 in the Living Bible says:

> *"Oh, don't worry, I wouldn't dare say that I am as wonderful as these other men who tell you how good they are! Their trouble is that they are only comparing themselves with each other and measuring themselves against their own little ideas. What stupidity!"*

I was raised in a Christian home ... with the best parents ever ... for that, I'm eternally grateful.

During high school and college ... I had a tendency to compare my behavior to that of my friends. I reasoned that I was okay spiritually because at least I wasn't doing what they were doing.

I came to realize that my standard for measurement shouldn't be the attitudes and actions of others ... but rather the Word of God.

4. **You're responsible for your actions and not those of anybody else.**

I've heard it said over the years ... that **you can't control what other people do, but you can control how you respond and react to what they do**.

Furthermore, you and you alone are accountable for your actions.

Amos 6:3 in the New Living Translation says:

> *"You push away every thought of coming disaster,*

> *but your actions only bring the day of judgment closer."*

Sadly, many believers will face a spiritual and eternal disaster because they've blamed others for what they did or didn't do.

I think Revelation 3:2 in the New Living Translation offers us some pretty good advice.

> *"Wake up! Strengthen what little remains, for even what is left is almost dead. I find that your actions do not meet the requirements of my God."*

Our actions reveal the depth of our faith and the strength of our character.

5. Comparing yourself to others limits your potential.

When you compare your performance and actions to that of another ... you are allowing them to set your standard of achievement. If your only goal is to do just a little better than someone else ... then you will never maximize your fullest potential.

Mark 9:23 in the GOD'S WORD Translation says:

> *"Jesus said to him, 'As far as possibilities go, everything is possible for the person who believes.' "*

This scripture doesn't say your success is dependent upon you doing what someone else does.

No, this scripture says that "everything is possible" for

the person who believes.

This passage is talking about you believing in somebody else ... it's referring to your belief in our great God Jehovah and knowing that all things are possible through Him.

<u>Your potential isn't limited by your actions but rather your beliefs</u>.

6. **Recognize and remember where your gifts and abilities originate.**

Romans 12:6 in the Message Bible says:

> *"Let's just go ahead and be what we were made to be, without enviously or pridefully comparing ourselves with each other, or trying to be something we aren't."*

According to James 1:17 every good and perfect gift comes from our Father in Heaven.

James 1:17 in the Amplified Bible says:

> *"Every good gift and every perfect (free, large, full) gift is from above; it comes down from the Father of all [that gives] light, in [the shining of] Whom there can be no variation [rising or setting] or shadow cast by His turning [as in an eclipse]."*

7. **You have guaranteed access to the greatest resource ever.**

As I was searching the scriptures and writing this teaching I came across a really powerful scripture. It's 1 Corinthians 4:7-8 in the Message Bible which says:

> *"For who do you know that really knows you, knows your heart? And even if they did, is there anything they would discover in you that you could take credit for? Isn't everything you have and everything you are sheer gifts from God? So what's the point of all this comparing and competing? You already have all you need. You already have more access to God than you can handle ..."*

I don't think a scripture could be any clearer. I strongly encourage you to write this scripture out on an index card, put it in your smart phone or other electronic gizmo so you can review it every day. It's a powerful word.

Just so ... we're clear ... **stop comparing yourself to other people.**

One more thing ... this just occurred to me. If you have brothers and/or sisters ... while growing up … you may have taunted each other with "Momma Likes You Best." Now that may be ... but I can give you an absolute fact ... GOD LIKES YOU BEST.

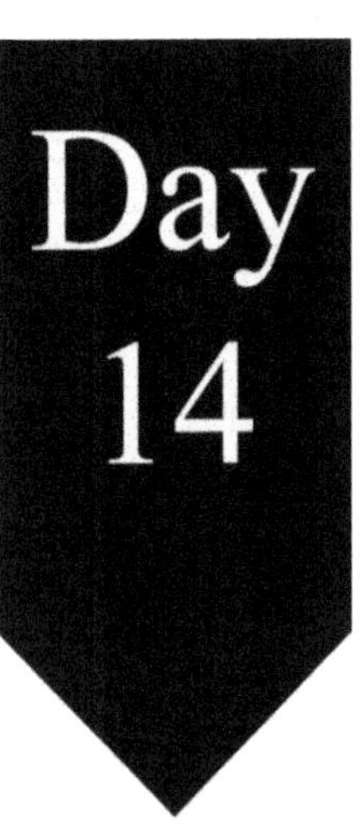

Ignorance Is a Choice

Ignorance is a choice. I'm absolutely convinced that the statement I just made is not only 100% factual but spiritually accurate as well.

Colossians 1:9 in the Amplified Bible says:

> *"For this reason we also, from the day we heard of it, have not ceased to pray and make [special] request for you, [asking] that you may be filled with the full (deep and clear) knowledge of His will in all spiritual wisdom [in comprehensive insight into the ways and purposes of God] and in understanding and discernment of spiritual things."*

Does that sound like He wants you to be ignorant … ABSOLUTELY NOT.

Here are eight reasons ignorance is a choice.

First, ignorance is simply ... a lack of knowledge.

If you ever read any of my teachings you know that ignorance is not knowing … whereas stupidity is knowing but choosing to ... ignore the information.

Speaking of stupidity ... there are some stupid laws on the books in the various states of this country. However, ignorance or a lack of knowledge of these laws is no excuse.

Consider some of these rather dumb, outdated or ridiculous laws.

It's illegal to wear a fake moustache that causes laughter in church in the State of Alabama.

It's illegal for donkeys to sleep in bathtubs in the State of Arizona.

It's illegal for men and women over the age of 18 to have less than one missing tooth visible when smiling in Tombstone, Arizona.

It's illegal for women to drive in a house coat in the state of California.

It's illegal for someone to shoot a buffalo from the second story of a hotel in Texas.

It's illegal in Carmel, New York, to go outside while wearing a jacket and pants that do not match.

Even when ridiculous, ignorance of these or other laws is no excuse.

Someone once said, "What you don't know can't hurt you." That's a lie for several reasons.

In the first place, **God knows it.**

In the second place, if your spouse is having an affair ... running up huge gambling debts or involved in something illegal ... **you may not know it but it can hurt you and your family.**

Second, if you lack knowledge, it's your fault because knowledge is available.

Acts 17:30 in the New International Version says:

> *"In the past God overlooked such ignorance, but now he commands all people everywhere to repent."*

God has overlooked ignorance in the past ... but He's not going to do so in the future. So He is commanding people everywhere to repent of their ignorance.

I think it's safe to say that if you have to repent of something ... that means you have sinned. By inference, logical interpretation and common sense ... it's a sin to be ignorant.

Third, God wants you to have knowledge.

There is absolutely no excuse for anyone to be ignorant about anything in the 21st century.

You can Google or Wikipedia any and every sort of information.

Of course, you have to use wisdom in putting value or faith in the search results you find.

Just because something is featured prominently on a search page doesn't mean that it's the truth, the whole truth and nothing but the truth ... but it can lead you to more knowledge through research.

If you don't own a computer ... go to the public library where you can use computers for free. However, **the greatest resource for knowledge in your life is not found in the stacks of your local library, but rather in the 66 chapters of your Bible.**

There is also no excuse for anyone not having a Bible, especially in the United States.

Romans 1:13 says:

> *"Now I would not have you ignorant, brethren, that oftentimes I purposed to come unto you, (but was let hitherto,) that I might have some fruit among you also, even as among other Gentiles."*

According to the Strong's Concordance the word *ignorance* means: "not knowing."

Simply said, *ignorance* is not knowing the facts. And as I said at the beginning of this message ... ***stupid*** **is knowing the facts but choosing not to do anything with or about that information and insight.**

Benjamin Franklin said, **"We are all born ignorant, but**

one must work hard to remain stupid."

There is a cure for *ignorance* ... get knowledge.

Fourth, making a decision without all the facts is ignorance.

Proverbs 18:13 says:

> *"He that answereth a matter before he heareth it, it is folly and shame unto him."*

Here's the Brother Harold translation of that verse.

"It's a sin to make a decision in ignorance when the facts are available."

The good news is that God will forgive you of ignorance ... which can be overcome by the gaining of knowledge.

Fifth, God wants ignorance silenced.

1 Peter 2:15 says:

> *"For so is the will of God, that with well doing ye may put to silence the ignorance of foolish men."*

God will not tolerate ignorance of any kind, and that is especially true of Him.

1 Corinthians 15:34 in the Message Bible says:

> *"Think straight. Awaken to the holiness of life. No*

> *more playing fast and loose with resurrection facts.* ***Ignorance of God is a luxury you can't afford in times like these.*** *Aren't you embarrassed that you've let this kind of thing go on as long as you have?"*

Sixth, ignorance will separate you from the love of God.

Ephesians 4:18 in the New International Version says:

> *"They are darkened in their understanding and separated from the life of God because of the ignorance that is in them due to the hardening of their hearts."*

1 Timothy 1:13 in the New International Version says:

> *"Even though I was once a blasphemer and a persecutor and a violent man, I was shown mercy because I acted in ignorance and unbelief."*

As I said earlier, wisdom delivers anyone from ignorance ... regardless of their personal situation or circumstances.

Seventh, knowledge leads to wisdom.

Hosea 4:6 is an indictment against the priests who were withholding knowledge from God's people. The scripture in the English Standard Version says:

> *"My people are destroyed for lack of knowledge;*

because you have rejected knowledge, I reject you from being a priest to me ..."

Knowledge is knowing and wisdom is putting the knowledge into practice to help you succeed. God wants His people walking in knowledge and wisdom.

James 1:5 in the Amplified Bible says:

"If any of you is deficient in wisdom, let him ask of the giving God [Who gives] to everyone liberally and ungrudgingly, without reproaching or fault-finding, and it will be given him."

Eighth, there is a significant financial reason why you shouldn't be ignorant but walk in knowledge and wisdom.

Ecclesiastes 9:16 in the Contemporary English Version says:

"So I decided that wisdom is better than strength. Yet if you are poor, no one pays any attention to you, no matter how smart you are."

Yes, wisdom is the principal thing ... but a wise, poor man is just that ... poor and no one will pay attention to him or her.

I think it's fair to say that knowledge leads to success … wisdom and wealth ... go hand in hand.

1 Kings 10:23 in the New Living Translation says:

> *"So King Solomon became richer and wiser than any other king on earth."*

Solomon chose wisdom and got riches ... we should do the same.

There are two scriptures I've shared with you several times during our RichThoughts for Breakfast calls ... but they bear repeating.

Ecclesiastes 7:11-12 in the Message Bible says:

> *"Wisdom is better when it's paired with money, especially if you get both while you're still living. Double protection: wisdom and wealth! Plus this bonus: Wisdom energizes its owner."*

Summing it all up … we've learned …

God doesn't want you ignorant ... because ignorance gets you nowhere ... it separates you from the love of God ... it's a result of not getting all the facts ... **you will never please God nor prosper as long as you remain ignorant.**

However, you don't have to remain ignorant ... because it's a choice ... make the choice to not remain ignorant.

8 Steps to the Good Life

Romans 16:20 in the Contemporary English Version says:

> "Then God, who gives peace, will soon crush Satan under your feet."

Have you ever wondered about the kind of life God wants you to live? The only way to know is to see what He says about it.

Proverbs 3:16-17 in the Living Bible translation says:

> *"Wisdom gives: a long, good life, riches, honor, pleasure, peace."*

Let's look at the five things wisdom gives you.

Wisdom gives:

1. a long, good life
2. riches
3. honor
4. pleasure
5. peace

Now you know why the Bible says "wisdom is the

principal thing." (Proverbs 4:7)

Proverbs 3:21 in the Living Bible says:

> *"Have two goals: wisdom—that is, knowing and doing right—and common sense. Don't let them slip away."*

Proverbs 4:10 in the Living Bible says:

> *"My child, listen to me and do as I say, and you will have a long, good life."*

Do you want a long, <u>good</u> life? **It's possible for you to move right now ... from the bondage and despair of debt ... to a lifestyle of financial freedom.**

Please understand that financial freedom is not based on how much you make … but how little you owe.

TODAY, RIGHT NOW, THIS VERY INSTANT ... purpose in your heart before God that you're ready to enjoy the good life He said you could have ... by being debt free and a blessing to all who know you.

Start your journey to the Debt Free lifestyle by following these eight simple points.

1. **Pray.**

Ask God to be at the center of your out-of-debt program … you will need His power to battle the forces wanting to keep you in debt.

Nehemiah 5:5 says:

> *"... we bring into bondage our sons and our daughters to be servants, and some of our daughters are brought unto bondage already: neither is it in our power to redeem them; for other men have our lands and vineyards."*

2. Know our God is a debt-canceling God.

In reading the remainder of Nehemiah 5, you'll see that the debt of the Israelites was canceled. If God did it for the children of Israel ... He will do it for you. He is no respecter of persons (Acts 10:34).

No matter how difficult your current financial situation may seem, there is nothing too difficult for YOUR GOD. Jeremiah 32:17 was not written by accident. It is meant to bring encouragement and hope into your life.

> *"Ah Lord God! behold, thou hast made the heaven and the earth by thy great power and stretched out arm, and there is nothing too hard for thee."*

But you've got a part to play.

3. Stop allowing the devil to trick you into impulse buying.

I'm sure you've seen or heard me quote Proverbs 21:20 in the Living Bible before … but it is worth repeating.

> *"The wise man saves for the future, but the foolish man spends whatever he gets."*

There was a song some years ago that goes something like … "GOT TO … GOT TO … HAVE IT." But the truth is … No … You Don't!

A bargain is not a bargain ... if you can't afford to pay for it.

4. Gang up on bills.

Organize your bills … pay off small bills first. Then use the money you were paying on them to gang up on a larger bill.

Think about it. If you can pay off a small bill in 3 months, you can add that money to the next bill and pay it off 6 months early, then add both those payments to your next bill and pay off the entire bill … the snowball effect will have you out of debt in no time!

NEVER, EVER pay off a bill and replace the payment with another payment! That one act will insure that you never get out of debt … period … paragraph.

5. Know where your money is going.

For over 20 years, I've taught people to get a spiral notebook and for the next 30 days track where they're spending every single penny of their money.

However, technology has made things easier ... if you have an iPhone, download the free app, "Easy Spending Expense Tracker." If you have an Android phone ... download the free app, "Expense Tracker."

Assign a category to each entry, such as, eating out. If you're married, both spouses should be a part of this process. You know where the big money is going, but you will be amazed at where the small money goes. Once you know where your money is going then you can redirect funds to your out of debt plan.

Track every cent you spend. If you buy a soft drink a day at $1.00 ... you will spend $365 during the course of the year. Could that extra $31 a month go toward ganging up on a debt?

As long as you're in debt, your money belongs to someone else. Get mad at debt and get those creditors off your back. God wants to help you do it.

6. Stop using or cut up the credit cards.

There are a lot of believers who need plastic surgery, but not on their double chins. Last year credit card companies collected over $25 BILLION dollars on just two fees ... late charges and exceeding credit limits.

Keep one credit card for emergencies. **Money is an excellent servant but a terrible master.** Let money work for you instead of you working for the money. Get a plan in motion so your money can be yours again.

7. Avoid dining out.

If you're so busy you don't have time to cook at home … at least order carry out … you will save the cost of the drinks plus 18-20% in tips.

Use coupons.

"Would you like to 'Biggie size' your combo meal?"

The answer should be an emphatic "NO." If you biggie size your combo meal three times a week ... that's $1.50 per week or $78 a year. You could use that money to be paying off a debt and relieving some of the financial pressure.

When my wife was gone all day, she used the crock pot or put frozen meat in the oven and programmed it to turn on at 3 PM in the afternoon so when we walked in the door at 6, dinner was almost ready. Be creative. Where there's a will, there's a way.

8. Find inexpensive recreational activities.

There are games other than video and computer games … board games don't have to be boring games … card games … trips to the park … Frisbee throwing … fishing in a local lake or pond …

Dollar Theater instead of first run movies … or discounts before 6 …

Movie a week … family of 3 @ $8 = $1,248 … go before 6 and save $312 a year …

Go to the dollar theater on Tuesday night … save $1,170 …

Think creatively … the answer doesn't have to be sitting in

front of the television …

Celebrate your victories.

Praise God for bills being paid off … for the blessings that are flowing.

When Saul questioned why David thought he could slay Goliath … David recalled his past victories … even small victories encourage our faith.

1 Samuel 17:34-36 says:

> *"And David said unto Saul, Thy servant kept his father's sheep, and there came a lion, and a bear, and took a lamb out of the flock: And I went out after him, and smote him, and delivered it out of his mouth: and when he arose against me, I caught him by his beard, and smote him, and slew him. Thy servant slew both the lion and the bear: and this uncircumcised Philistine shall be as one of them, seeing he hath defied the armies of the living God."*

In your journey to the Debt Free lifestyle ... you need to develop your own "Did I ever tell you about the time" testimony.

David went after the lion and the bear that was attacking something that were precious to him ... that's what you've got to do in order to activate these 8 steps ... you've got to press forward until the **GOOD LIFE is yours to enjoy.**

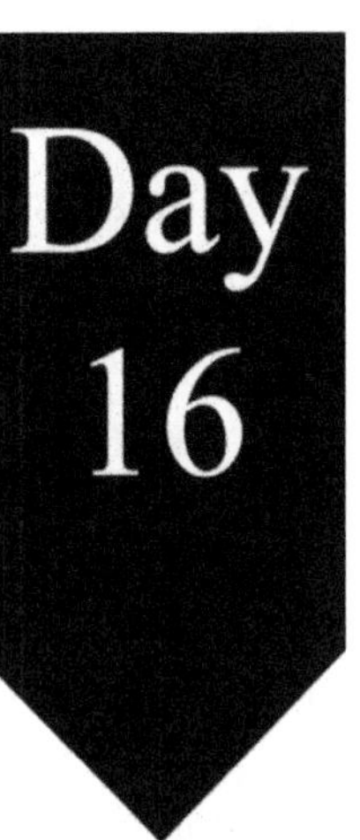

The Dynamic Duo

It's a beautiful Sunday morning ... even though the window shades in my office are closed and I have no idea what the weather is like outside ... I know one thing for certain ... it's a Spectacular Sunday.

The beauty of this day is not in whether the sun is shining, it's pouring rain or there's snow on the ground ... the majesty of Sunday is that we get to spend time with Him and His other children.

Every Sunday morning in church is like attending a family reunion ... where we energize our faith and confidence in Him ... as well as loving on the saints.

This morning I found myself reading Jeremiah 17:7 in the Amplified Bible which says:

> *"[Most] blessed is the man who believes in, trusts in, and relies on the Lord, and whose hope and confidence the Lord is."*

I suggest you personalize this verse and let it sink in.

> *"[Most] blessed is [Your Name] who believes in, trusts in, and relies on the Lord, and whose hope*

> *and confidence the Lord is."*

What makes a person blessed? The Word says that a person is blessed "… whose hope and confidence is in the Lord …"

Where does confidence come from?

Can you gain confidence by reading the Bible or a motivational book? Yes.

Can you gain confidence by listening to your parents or the right mentors? Yes.

But the real question is ... **where do we find a source of confidence that never changes ... is not moved by our actions or circumstances?**

Psalm 71:5 in the Amplified Bible says:

> *"For You are my hope; O Lord God, You are my trust from my youth and the source of my confidence."*

God can and wants to be the source of our confidence.

Blessed is the person whose faith and confidence is in the Lord.

If I were to ask you who's the Dynamic Duo ... you would probably say "Batman and Robin," especially if you keep up with popular culture.

However, the real forces for truth and justice give us a power that surpasses the superheroes of comic book fame.

Our Dynamic Duo is "Faith and Confidence."

Luke 17:19 in the Amplified Bible says:

> *"And He said to him, Get up and go on your way. Your faith (your trust and confidence that spring from your belief in God) has restored you to health."*

Faith and confidence bring healing.

Your faith produces a spiritual confidence. Continued faith building produces solid rock confidence.

Luke 5:20 in the Amplified Bible says:

> *"And when He saw [their confidence in Him, springing from] their faith, He said, Man, your sins are forgiven you!"*

Your faith and confidence bring forgiveness of sins.

Not only that ... your faith and confidence will sustain you in the midst of adversity.

Psalm 56:3 in the Amplified Bible says:

> *"What time I am afraid, I will have confidence in and put my trust and reliance in You."*

The scripture is clear ... **we're blessed, forgiven, healed and protected when our faith and confidence is in Him.** Fears flee when confidence shows up.

Jeremiah 17:8 in the Amplified Bible says:

> "*For he shall be like a tree planted by the waters that spreads out its roots by the river; and it shall not see and fear when heat comes; but its leaf shall be green. It shall not be anxious and full of care in the year of drought, nor shall it cease yielding fruit.*"

When we put our trust, faith and confidence in Him, we're like a strong tree planted by the river. I find it interesting that this verse says we *"shall not see and fear when the heat comes ..."*

What's the heat in your life?

When you've lost your job ... and you're not sure where the next meal for your family is coming from ... that's a heat that can certainly produce fear.

When you've gotten so far behind in your payments that you're afraid to answer the phone because of collection agencies ... that brings a financial heat that causes fear.

When the doctor uses the "C" word and tells you it's inoperable ... that produces the fear and brings the heat.

Whatever situation you're facing ... take heart in knowing that the fear and heat may come into your life ... but your leaf which the scripture describes ... the leaf that represents the vitality and viability of who you are ... will not fade and drop off the tree.

I will confess to you that biology was not one of my strongest subjects … in high school … or college … but I do know that a healthy green leaf … represents vibrant life.

I think it's also important to take note of the remainder of Jeremiah 17:8:

> "... *It shall not be anxious and full of care in the year of drought, nor shall it cease yielding fruit.*"

As long as you have your trust, faith and confidence in Him ... you shouldn't be anxious about anything.

Matthew 6:27 in the Amplified Bible says:

> *"And who of you by worrying and being anxious can add one unit of measure (cubit) to his stature or to the span of his life?"*

The Contemporary English Version of Matthew 6:27 says:

> *"Can worry make you live longer?"*

Philippians 4:6 in the Amplified Bible says:

> *"Do not fret or have any anxiety about anything, but in every circumstance and in everything, by prayer and petition (definite requests), with*

> *thanksgiving, continue to make your wants known to God."*

When everyone else around you is singing the financial blues ... you need to be in the P & P mode ... Praying and Praising. Truthfully, that's another pretty dynamic duo.

You may be in the midst of a financial drought ... your sales may be down, but you shall not cease yielding fruit ... being productive in the marketplace ... or providing a proper income for your family.

You may have a tendency to wonder and worry about your retirement and investment income, which has all but vanished ... but you've got to know that you will continue producing fruit that will replenish your supply.

And by the way, "wonder and worry" are the bad guys that can be taken down by either of the dynamic duos ... faith and confidence … and prayer and praising.

When you're rooted and grounded in Him ... the winds, waves and fires of adversity may come against you ... but they will not prevail.

Some of the best advice I can give you is found in Matthew 6:34 in the Message Bible:

> *"Give your entire attention to what God is doing right now, and don't get worked up about what may or may not happen tomorrow. God will help you deal with whatever hard things come up when the time comes."*

The key to your success ... your ability to overcome whatever comes your way ... is found in your relationship with the Dynamic Duos of Faith and Confidence … and Prayer and Praising.

Once again, God is giving us a clear prescription on how to live the good life.

Here's a bit of Herring humor to liven up your morning …

Q: Why don't you iron 4-Leaf clovers?
A: Because you don't want to press your luck.

Jokes aside, remember … **God's Dynamic Duo can overcome every bad thing in our lives …**

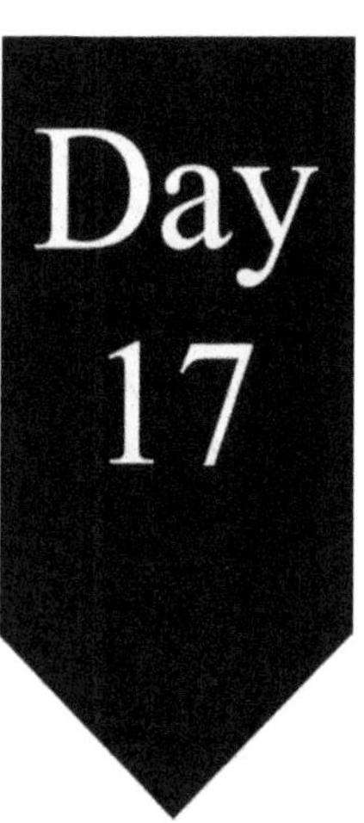

7 "In's" That Leave You Without

Recently, I got happy in the Lord while eating at an In-N-Out Burger location. Unless you live in California, Nevada, Arizona, Utah or Texas ... you'll probably not be familiar with this fast food chain.

At the time, In-N-Out Burger had been operating in Texas for only a short time, even though the company was founded in 1948.

Now let me share with you why I got happy ... it wasn't just because of the food … but I had been told that the people who own the company are Christians and that John 3:16 is written on the bottom of all the drink cups ... and it is ... you guessed it ... that was what made me happy.

So you might say I had a happy meal at someplace other than McDonald's.

As I was thinking about the term In-N-Out ... I realized there are seven "in's" that will leave you without ... experiencing God's best.

1. Indifferent

We should never be indifferent about our salvation, because it's what took us out of Satan's camp and put us on the highway to heaven.

Hebrews 2:3 in the Living Bible says:

> *"What makes us think that we can escape if we are indifferent to this great salvation announced by the Lord Jesus himself and passed on to us by those who heard him speak?"*

God never wants us to be indifferent to the plight of others ... instead He wants us making a difference.

Hebrews 6:12 in the Living Bible says:

> *"Then, knowing what lies ahead for you, you won't become bored with being a Christian nor become spiritually dull and indifferent, but **you will be anxious to follow the example of those who receive all that God has promised them because of their strong faith and patience.**"*

When we remove the "in" from indifferent we will be ... different than them. If we want to be the salt of the earth ... then we need to STOP ACTING LIKE THEM … ***S.A.L.T.*** … ***S-TOP A-CTING L-IKE T-HEM.***

2. Inaccurate

God does not tolerate things that are inaccurate in our personal lives or in our businesses.

Micah 6:11 in the GOD'S WORD Translation says:

> *"I cannot tolerate dishonest scales and bags filled with inaccurate weights."*

When you remove the "in" from inaccurate, you become accurate ... which is what God always wants.

Titus 2:8 in the GOD'S WORD Translation says:

> *"Speak an accurate message that cannot be condemned. Then those who oppose us will be ashamed because they cannot say anything bad about us."*

If you're always accurate ... if you always tell the truth ... no slander against you will ever take root and grow ... rather it will dry up, dissolve, disappear and be exposed for what it is.

3. Inadequate

1 Corinthians 2:3-5 in the Message Bible says:

> *"I was unsure of how to go about this, and felt totally inadequate—I was scared to death, if you want the truth of it—and so nothing I said could have impressed you or anyone else. But the Message came through anyway. God's Spirit and God's power did it, which made it clear* ***that your life of faith is a response to God's power****, not to some fancy mental or emotional footwork by me or anyone else."*

When we try to do things on our own ... our efforts will always be inadequate.

When we realize we have the authority and power ... physical and mental strength and ability over all the

power of the enemy ... we will never feel inadequate another day in our life.

Acts 1:8 says:

> *"But ye shall receive power, after that the Holy Ghost is come upon you: and ye shall be witnesses unto me both in Jerusalem, and in all Judaea, and in Samaria, and unto the uttermost part of the earth."*

When we remove the "in" from inadequate ... we will always be more than adequate for every challenge as we follow the unction of the Holy Spirit.

4. Inconsistent

Inconsistency in our faith or the character of our friends is extremely dangerous to both our future well-being and prosperity.

2 Corinthians 6:14 in the Amplified Bible says:

> *"Do not be unequally yoked with unbelievers [do not make mismated alliances with them or come under a different yoke with them, inconsistent with your faith]. For what partnership have right living and right standing with God with iniquity and lawlessness? Or how can light have fellowship with darkness?"*

Sadly, our greatest times of being consistent in our faith are when there's trouble on the horizon. When things are peaceful and normal ... we sometimes become inconsistent in our faith, because we're taking things for granted.

Remember this saying: **"Inconsistency Feeds Your Doubts."**

God showed me that inconsistency is the trick, trap and lie ... the devil uses to rob God's children of their blessings and inheritance.

When we remove the "in" from inconsistency we become consistent.

5. Inaccessible

I praise God every day ... that He's not now ... nor has He ever been ... nor will He ever be inaccessible to us.

Dictionary.com defines inaccessible as:

"not accessible; unapproachable."

I rejoice that we serve a God that is accessible to us ... 24/7.

Job 28:12 in GOD'S WORD Translation says:

> *"[Wisdom Is Inaccessible to Decay and Death] Where can wisdom be found? Where does understanding live?"*

When you fully understand your benefit package as a born-again child of God ... you know that you have unlimited access to the King of Kings and Lord of Lords.

Psalm 86:7 says:

> *"In the day of my trouble I will call upon thee: for thou wilt answer me."*

Jeremiah 29:12-14 in the Amplified Bible says:

> *"Then you will call upon Me, and you will come and pray to Me, and I will hear and heed you. Then you will seek Me, inquire for, and require Me [as a vital necessity] and find Me when you search for Me with all your heart. I will be found by you, says the Lord, and I will release you from captivity ..."*

When we remove the "in" from inaccessible ... we will be accessible to every blessing of God ... and have access to important people.

6. Insincere

Nobody likes a phony ... someone who is insincere. You know the type ... always blowing smoke at you.

You may tolerate the insincere, but God doesn't. Sadly, there are even some Christians who fall into this category.

Philippians 1:17 in the Amplified Bible says:

> *"But the former preach Christ out of a party spirit, insincerely [out of no pure motive, but thinking to annoy me], supposing they are making my bondage more bitter and my chains more galling."*

God warns us about people who are insincere ... who use flattery to get what they want.

Proverbs 7:21 in the New Living Translation says:

> *"So she seduced him with her pretty speech and enticed him with her flattery."*

According to dictionary.com the word flattery is defined as:

"a flattering compliment or speech; excessive, insincere praise."

God always wants you and me motivated by sincere reasons ... not for personal gain at the expense of the Gospel.

When we remove the "in" from insincere we become sincere about God's plan for our lives.

7. Inactive

God is looking for people who are full of fire and the Holy Ghost.

God is looking for people who will get up off what's been holding them back and actively pursue the vision He has given them.

James 2:20 in the Amplified Bible says:

> *"Are you willing to be shown [proof], you foolish (unproductive, spiritually deficient) fellow, that faith apart from [good] works is inactive and ineffective and worthless?"*

Your faith is what will prompt you to a new level of kingdom action.

<u>**God's greatest desire is for you to be His new action hero**</u> ... someone who defies all odds to become victorious

against the forces of evil. I believe ... He's looking for you.

One final thought …

You must get rid of the seven "in's" if you ever want to be out … standing in God's eyes.

7 Bad Decisions You Should Avoid

Hebrews 13:5 in the New Living Translation says:

> *"... For God has said, 'I will never fail you. I will never abandon you.' "*

You can personalize Hebrews 13:5 like this:

> *"... For God has said, 'I will never fail [Name]. I will never abandon [Name].' "*

God will never abandon you, but you may still reap the consequences for decisions you made.

Associating with evil people can dramatically alter the course of our lives. Evil relationships precipitate bad judgments.

In 2 Chronicles 18 there are seven clear examples of how Jehoshaphat ignored his most important relationship … alliance … partnership … the one with His God. Here are seven bad decisions you can learn to avoid right now.

1. Being Unequally Yoked

Jehoshaphat made a huge mistake.

2 Chronicles 18:1 in the New Living Translation says:

> *"Jehoshaphat enjoyed great riches and high esteem, and he made an alliance with Ahab of Israel by having his son marry Ahab's daughter."*

Do you know what happens if a righteous person marries a sinful person ... they will have Rosemary's Baby. **Mixing righteousness with sin does not make the sin righteous!**

2 Corinthians 6:14 says:

> *"Be ye not unequally yoked together with unbelievers: for what fellowship hath righteousness with unrighteousness? and what communion hath light with darkness?"*

In the Strong's Concordance the phrase *unequally yoked together* in the Greek (G2086) means:

"to come under an unequal or different yoke; to have fellowship with one who is not an equal."

Unbelievers are definitely not equal to believers.

I Corinthians 2:14 in the New Living Translation says:

> *"But people who aren't spiritual can't receive these truths from God's Spirit. It all sounds foolish to them and they can't understand it, for only those who are spiritual can understand what the Spirit means."*

How frustrating would it be to love someone who does not understand the language you speak?

The New English Translation of 2 Corinthians 6:14 says:

> *"Do not become partners with those who do not believe, for what partnership is there between righteousness and lawlessness, or what fellowship does light have with darkness?"*

When Jehoshaphat offered his son in marriage to the daughter of King Ahab, he became unequally yoked with a wicked man.

2. Forming an Unholy Alliance Without Asking God First

2 Chronicles 18:3 in the Amplified Bible says:

> *"Ahab king of Israel said to Jehoshaphat king of Judah, Will you go with me to Ramoth-gilead? He answered, I am as you are, and my people as your people; we will be with you in the war."*

God will never bless what He hasn't approved.

After Jehoshaphat agreed to the unholy alliance ... then he suggested they ask God for His approval.

2 Chronicles 18:4 in the Amplified Bible says:

> *"And Jehoshaphat said to the king of Israel, Inquire first, I pray you, for the word of the Lord today."*

There are some people who, using the wisdom of the world, think it's better to ask for forgiveness rather than ask for permission. The worldly logic says that if you ask for permission and don't get it ... then you're bound to not take action.

However, if you take action ... and make someone unhappy, then you can ask for forgiveness.

This type of twisted logic will not be accepted on Judgment Day.

3. Letting a Poor Self Image Cause You To Underestimate Yourself and/or Over-Estimate Someone Else

2 Chronicles 18:3 in the Amplified Bible says:

> *"... He answered, I am as you are, and my people as your people; we will be with you in the war."*

Not seeing yourself the way God sees you can only lead to trouble. It will cause you to doubt your self-worth which will cause you to embrace and tolerate harmful relationships.

A woman who was abused as a child frequently makes bad choices in relationships because she has no self-worth. It's only the grace of God that saves these women from a life of abuse and co-dependency on abusive spouses or boyfriends.

The best way to create a positive self-image and avoid ungodly relationships is to realize just how important you are to God and how He desires your obedience to His Word.

4. Finding an Expert Witness for the Defense

Have you ever watched any of the television shows where each legal defense team is trying to find a credible eyewitness who will agree with their side of the story?

In most of these TV programs ... the expert witnesses generally are looking for a payday ... what they can get out of it.

If you've made a stupid mistake ... it's human nature to seek someone who will collaborate your testimony and the dumb decisions you've already made.

Jehoshaphat knows things are not progressing in a godly manner ... so in 2 Chronicles 18:6 in the Amplified Bible he says:

> *"But Jehoshaphat said, 'Is there not another prophet of the Lord here by whom we may inquire?' "*

King Ahab immediately pooh-poohs Jehoshaphat's suggestion because he knows from past experience that God's prophet will not play his games.

King Ahab is looking for someone who will agree with everything he wants to do.

5. Compromising Your Principles Rather Than Your Procedures

A lack of personal, moral and spiritual commitment will cause you to compromise ... to fall for a trick of the enemy.

If you want to lead a joyful life ... then don't compromise with evil ... regardless of the form in which it manifests itself.

Psalm 119:2-3 in the New Living Translation says:

> *"Joyful are those who obey his laws and search for him with all their hearts. They do not compromise with evil, and they walk only in his paths."*

There is an old saying **that if you don't stand for something, you will fall for anything.**

6. Remaining Ignorant or Stupid ... Either Way It's Dangerous

I think being unequally yoked will open up a person to all sorts of spiritual sin and cloud a person's good sense.

2 Chronicles 18:28-29 in the New Living Translation says:

> *"... The king of Israel said to Jehoshaphat, 'As we go into battle, I will disguise myself so no one will recognize me, but you wear your royal robes.' So the king of Israel disguised himself, and they went into battle."*

As I've read these two verses over the years, I've often wondered if Jehoshaphat was a hamburger short of a Happy Meal or just naïve and gullible.

In military battles ... it's common knowledge and a strategy of warfare to kill the leader (king) thus demoralizing the remaining forces into surrender or retreat.

So you would think that Jehoshaphat was smart enough to realize what Ahab was suggesting when he asked him to go into battle wearing his royal robes.

In essence, Jehoshaphat was figuratively painting a bull's eye on his back. In fact, a reading of 2 Chronicles 18:30-32 will reveal that Jehoshaphat would have been killed except that the Lord saved him.

Once again, when you're unequally yoked ... you open yourself to every deception of the enemy and those he uses to do his bidding.

7. Running From Conflict

I will confess to you that I don't like conflict ... never have … probably never will.

I realize there are some people who thrive on conflict ... who enjoy the sting of battle ... I'm not one of them.

Yet, while I don't like conflict ... I will not run from it, especially if it violates my spiritual sense of right and wrong.

Have you ever noticed people who always have to be right … who want to have the last word in every conversation or disagreement?

It's a matter of pride ... and misplaced values.

Proverbs 13:10 in the New Living Translation says:

> *"Pride leads to conflict; those who take advice are wise."*

A final word … before we condemn Jehoshaphat too soundly ... perhaps we need to consider our own lives ... the times that we've been unequally yoked ... or even worse, the times that we've forgotten how our great God Jehovah has delivered us from every adversity.

That's just … something to think about.

5 Ways to Keep Yourself Thinking Rich Thoughts

It's amazing how certain totally useless pieces of information are stored in our mental hard drives.

This morning as I read Joshua 8:1 the phrase "fear not" stirred in me. Those two words "fear not" appear 62 times in the King James Version of the Bible.

Suddenly, a bit of popular culture trivia flashed through my mind.

I recalled the phrase, "Be afraid. Be very afraid."

As I wondered where that phrase came from ... I remembered it was from a movie I'd seen sometime in the past, although truthfully, I couldn't recall the movie's name.

A quick Google search revealed the quote was from a science fiction movie I saw in 1986 … many years ago, but it had become programmed into my subconscious mind. <u>It made me wonder just how much other basically useless or even contrary information is programmed in my mind</u>.

We all need to be mindful of the things that we allow to enter our mental thought processes. Not only that … but we need to take dominion over the thoughts we allow to reappear in our minds.

Which brings me to another question ...

Have you ever seen a really bad movie? Did you walk out in the middle, or did you just leave after it finished, disgusted because the movie was bad, depressing or just not worth two hours of your life?

I've walked out of my share of movies … sometimes even getting my money back from a sympathetic theater manager.

Let me say, that **if you're offended by what you see in a movie, just think how the Holy Spirit feels.**

Here's the question … if you ever saw a really bad movie … would you go see it again?

Your answer is probably an unqualified and resolute "NO."

I think we've established by now that most people would never go see a really bad movie again. We've also established the fact that we don't want to replay the negative images in our mind ... again.

Yet way too many believers are replaying negative, hurtful, offensive things in their minds time after time, day after day, year after year.

Way too often **we're retrieving things from our mental hard drives that we need to kill with the Sword of the Spirit and bury … for good!**

I'm going to share five ways to take control of your thought life and keep thinking Rich Thoughts.

1. Ask: Where Did That Come From?

It's almost impossible for us to totally filter the thoughts and mental images to which we're exposed on a daily basis.

A number of studies point out that the average American is exposed to over 3,000 advertising messages a day ... this includes radio, TV, Internet, billboards or any other medium that promotes a product, cause or lifestyle.

Assuming that you sleep eight hours a day … that means that during the other sixteen hours a day ... you are exposed to over 3.5 advertising messages every minute of the day. During the year you will be exposed to 1,095,000 advertising messages.

By the way, it grieves me to say that seldom is there an intelligent commercial … most of them are geared to the base, the vain, or the greedy side of human nature.

That's why it's so essential that you guard what you receive in your mental hard drive.

If it doesn't line up with God's thoughts, ideas and commandments, it is our responsibility to purposely cast it down so it's not detrimental to our Christian growth.

2 Corinthians 10:5 says:

> *"Casting down imaginations, and every high thing that exalteth itself against the knowledge of God, and bringing into captivity every thought to the obedience of Christ."*

The Amplified Bible translation of the verse says:

> *"... we lead every thought and purpose away captive into the obedience of Christ (the Messiah, the Anointed One) ..."*

Notice the verse says that "we" lead.

You and I determine the thoughts we are willing to receive on a moment-by-moment basis and also what we do with them. **We must purpose to only receive the right kind of thoughts.** Our consciousness of what's happening will allow greater vigilance on our part.

2. Evaluate Incoming Thoughts

The second step to taking control of your thoughts is to evaluate and analyze the thoughts that you're receiving.

Let's look at 2 Corinthians 10:5 in the Amplified Bible once again. It says:

> *"[Inasmuch as we] refute arguments and theories and reasonings and every proud and lofty thing that*

> *sets itself up against the [true] knowledge of God; and we lead every thought and purpose away captive into the obedience of Christ ..."*

In order to be successful in everyday life ... we MUST take captive (make our prisoner) every thought that comes to our minds ... evaluate and analyze it. We compare its obedience (or lack of obedience) to God's will in our life so we know whether to reject or accept it.

3. Decide to Receive or Reject

When confronted with a thought, idea or suggestion, regardless of its origin ... you must decide whether to receive, accept or reject the new visitor.

One of the hardest things for believers to understand is that some of the thoughts, ideas and suggestions are from some very well-meaning family members and friends who may not realize what they say is wrong.

If we ever begin to entertain any bad, evil or negative thoughts, ideas or suggestions ... then we're allowing them to build the wrong type of stronghold in our lives.

Strongholds are a collection/grouping of thoughts, ideas and suggestions. If your stronghold is not based in the Word, it will cause you to act on information that is wrong. **Error leads to more error because you are building on something you think is truth when in fact it is not.**

Every believer has the authority to use God's Word to

reject thoughts and ideas the enemy wants to use against us.

4. Replace What God Casts Out

It's not enough to cast down imaginations … you must begin to replace those negative thoughts that you've previously had (notice that I said previously) … with truth from the Word of God.

The void must be filled, and God is waiting for our response.

1 Chronicles 28:9 in the New Living Translation says:

> *"And Solomon, my son, learn to know the God of your ancestors intimately. Worship and serve him with your whole heart and a willing mind. For the Lord sees every heart and knows every plan and thought. If you seek him, you will find him. But if you forsake him, he will reject you forever."*

His desire is for the right kind of thoughts to be in our minds. Rich thoughts allow God to manifest good things in our lives.

5. Renew Ourselves by God's Power

Romans 12:2 in the Amplified Bible says:

> *"Do not be conformed to this world (this age), [fashioned after and adapted to its external, superficial customs], but be transformed (changed)*

> *by the [entire] renewal of your mind [by its new ideals and its new attitude], so that you may prove [for yourselves] what is the good and acceptable and perfect will of God, even the thing which is good and acceptable and perfect [in His sight for you]."*

In the New Living Translation the verse says:

> *"... let God transform you into a new person by changing the way you think. Then you will learn to know God's will for you, which is good and pleasing and perfect."*

If we want God to transform us ... then we need to change the way we think and what we think about.

When a computer gets cluttered with random bits of information scattered on its hard-drive ... it slows the speed. The solution is to defrag (remove) all of the irrelevant information.

Maybe it's time to run a diagnostic on your mental hard drive.

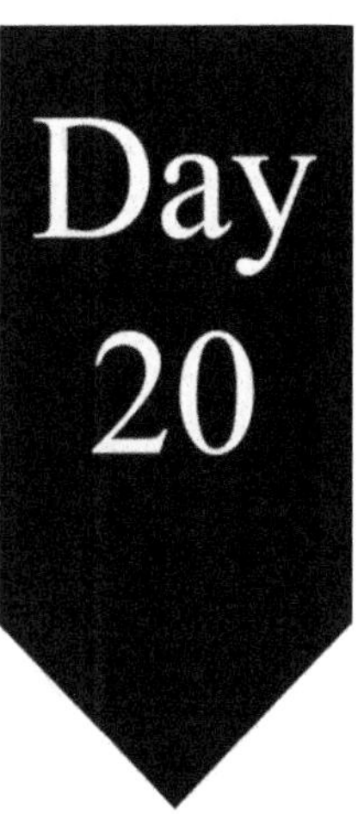

11 Ways To Handle Tough Times

I remember where I was standing the day the Lord said to me ...

"Tell my children to stop calling these days tough times."

What does the Word of God say about tough times? Has His message, advice, promises or Word ever changed?

Absolutely NOT.

Hebrews 13:8 says:

> *"Jesus Christ the same yesterday, and to day, and for ever."*

As I was meditating on what the Lord had spoken to me ... He led me to a scripture of the Bible that I hadn't read in a long time ... Nahum 1:7 in the Message Bible.

> *"God is good, a hiding place in **tough times.** He recognizes and welcomes anyone looking for help, No matter how desperate the trouble ..."*

God is our refuge ... our hiding place ... He will protect all who seek Him and free them from every attack of the enemy.

God should be and wants to be a constant source of inspiration and protection for us from the moment we draw our first breath until we're with Him in glory.

When I asked our Heavenly Father how people should respond to tough times, He led me to 2 Corinthians 6:1-8, 10 in the Message Bible:

> *"Companions as we are in this work with you, we beg you, please don't squander one bit of this marvelous life God has given us. God reminds us, I heard your call in the nick of time; The day you needed me, I was there to help.*
>
> *"Well, now is the right time to listen, the day to be helped. Don't put it off; don't frustrate God's work by showing up late, throwing a question mark over everything we're doing. Our work as God's servants gets validated—or not—in the details.*
>
> *"People are watching us as we stay at our post, alertly, unswervingly ... in* ***hard times, tough times, bad times*** *... working hard, working late, working without eating; with pure heart, clear head, steady hand; in gentleness, holiness, and honest love; when we're telling the truth, and when God's showing his power; when we're doing our best setting things right; when we're praised, and when we're blamed; slandered, and honored; true to our word, though distrusted; ignored by the world, but recognized by God; terrifically alive ... enriching many; having nothing, having it all."*

As I read and reread this verse ... the Lord showed me 11 ways that you and I need to handle times that the world is calling "tough."

1. **You're not alone.**

Hebrews 13:5 in the Message Bible says:

*"... I'll **never** let you down, **never** walk off and **leave** you."*

Personalize that with your name …

*"... I'll **never** let [Your Name] down, **never** walk off and **leave** [Your Name]."*

2. **Don't squander or waste one minute of the life God has given you.**

Ephesians 5:11-16 in the Message Bible says:

"Don't waste your time on useless work, mere busywork, the barren pursuits of darkness. Expose these things for the sham they are. It's a scandal when people waste their lives on things they must do in the darkness where no one will see. Rip the cover off those frauds and see how attractive they look in the light of Christ.

"Wake up from your sleep, Climb out of your coffins; Christ will show you the light! So watch your step. Use your head. Make the most of every

chance you get. These are desperate times!"

Do you have a plan for today? If not, your day has a plan for you.

3. **God will respond to you when you call on Him.**

2 Chronicles 15:3-4 in the Message Bible says:

"... God will stick with you as long as you stick with him. If you look for him he will let himself be found; but if you leave him he'll leave you. For a long time Israel didn't have the real God, nor did they have the help of priest or teacher or book. But when they were in trouble and got serious, and decided to seek God, the God of Israel, God let himself be found."

4. **He will always be there to help you.**

For those who say ... they're all alone ... may I suggest you read and reread Psalm 139:1 in the Message Bible which says:

"God, investigate my life; get all the facts first-hand. I'm an open book to you; even from a distance, <u>you know what I'm thinking</u>. You know when I leave and when I get back; I'm never out of your sight. You know everything I'm going to say before I start the first sentence. I look behind me and you're there, then up ahead and you're there,

> *too—your reassuring presence, coming and going. This is too much, too wonderful—I can't take it all in!"*

Say with me ... **I'm never alone.**

5. Now is the time to listen to Him.

Deuteronomy 30:10 in the New Living Translation says:

> *"The Lord your God will delight in you if you obey his voice and keep the commands and decrees written in this Book of Instruction, and if you turn to the Lord your God with all your heart and soul."*

If there is one thing I want ... it's for God to delight in me. HALLELUJAH!!

6. Today is your day to receive His help.

Jeremiah 32:40 in the New Living Translation says:

> *"And I will make an everlasting covenant with them: I will never stop doing good for them. I will put a desire in their hearts to worship me, and they will never leave me."*

How can I know this is the day I will receive God's help ... in what I'm going through? Ask Him.

7. Don't delay doing the things that God speaks to you.

Ecclesiastes 5:4 in the New Living Translation says:

"When you make a promise to God, don't delay in following through, for God takes no pleasure in fools. Keep all the promises you make to him."

8. People are watching to see how you respond to His protection and direction.

Hebrews 12:1 in the Amplified Bible says:

"THEREFORE THEN, since we are surrounded by so great a cloud of witnesses [who have borne testimony to the Truth], let us strip off and throw aside every encumbrance (unnecessary weight) and that sin which so readily (deftly and cleverly) clings to and entangles us, and let us run with patient endurance and steady and active persistence the appointed course of the race that is set before us."

9. Get the victory over every possible attack of the enemy.

Exodus 14:13 in the New International Version says:

"Moses answered the people, 'Do not be afraid. Stand firm and you will see the ***deliverance*** *the LORD will bring you today. The Egyptians you see today you will never see again.' "*

10. Manifest everything God has for you.

Joshua 21:45 in the New Living Translation says:

> *"Not a single one of all the good promises the Lord had given to the family of Israel was left unfulfilled; everything he had spoken came true."*

Psalm 77:14 in the Living Bible says:

> *"You are the God of miracles and wonders! You still demonstrate your awesome power."*

11. Speak to your times.

Romans 4:17 in the Living Bible says:

> *"... And this promise is from God himself, who makes the dead live again and speaks of future events with as much certainty as though they were already past."*

When God told me to tell His children to stop calling the current situation "tough times," He was not telling us to ignore the situation. But rather, He was directing us to speak to the situations we want to create.

Hebrews 12:3 in the Message Bible offers some great advice when you need an energy boost. It says:

> *"When you find yourselves flagging in your faith, go over that story again, item by item, that long litany of hostility he plowed through. That will shoot adrenaline into your souls!"*

How do you handle tough times ... you know ... **just do it.**

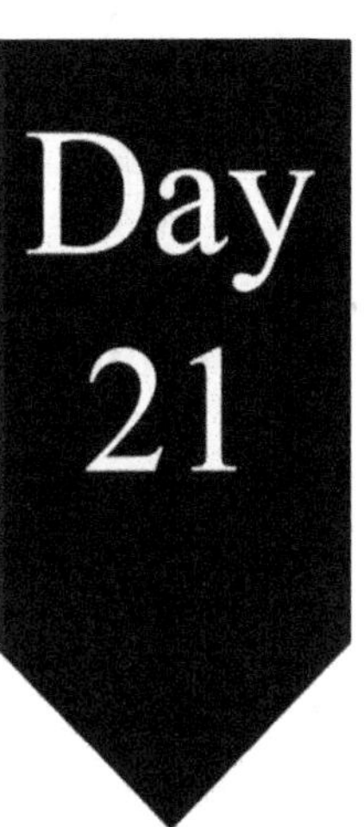

10 Things You Ought To Know

I'm going to make three absolute statements based on the Word of God.

First, when you give as God directs … you will prosper.

Second, when you follow God's instructions … you will be blessed.

Third, when and if you ever touch God's anointed … you sin against Him.

Some might ask how I can make such absolute statements ... it's easy ... because they're backed up in the Word of God.

Let's look at 2 Chronicles 24 where we will discover at least ten powerful truths in this story of Joash, the boy who became king.

1. **You're not destined to failure, or for that matter, success based on who your parents are or aren't.**

I've heard people attribute their lack of success or failures to their parents, teachers, employers and the list goes on ...

basically, to anyone and everyone but themselves.

There comes a point when you become accountable for your own life ... because you realize that your excuses don't cut it anymore.

Joash's grandmother was Athaliah, and she was one evil queen. She killed the royal family and would have killed Joash if she could have found him. However, he was hidden in the temple by his aunt, the wife of Jehoiada, the High priest.

The success of Joash was not based on his family but His God and mentor, which leads us to the second point.

2. **Your success in life is frequently determined by who you listen to and the advice you receive.**

Joash was not only protected and taught by Jehoiada … he was positioned for success because of the efforts of the High Priest who involved the military in a plan to restore him as the rightful King.

2 Chronicles 24:2 says:

> *"And Joash did that which was right in the sight of the LORD all the days of Jehoiada the priest."*

3. **God is not pleased when you aren't giving to His work as you've been directed to.**

2 Chronicles 24:4-6 in the Message Bible says:

> *"The time came when Joash determined to renovate The Temple of God. He got the priests and Levites together and said, 'Circulate through the towns of Judah every year and collect money from the people to repair The Temple of your God. You are in charge of carrying this out.' But the Levites dragged their feet and didn't do anything."*

Disobedience to His instructions and those in authority over us ... does not make God happy.

4. **God is not happy when you spend His money on things instead of tithes and offerings.**

2 Chronicles 24:7 in the New Living Translation says:

> *"Over the years the followers of wicked Athaliah had broken into the Temple of God, and they had used all the dedicated things from the Temple of the Lord to worship the images of Baal."*

You may be breathing a sigh of relief because you don't give God's money to idols. However, I need to ask you a question.

Are you giving your tithes and offerings ... or is that money sitting in your closet in the form of designer clothes or parked in your driveway in the form of a new car or taking up one wall in your living room as a High Def Flat Panel TV?

Truly, any and everything that you put before the Lord's tithes and offerings will be detrimental to your financial and spiritual health.

5. **When King Joash began to stress giving ... "all" the people followed their leader and everybody gave. Not only that, but they were happy in their giving.**

A good leadership example is important in giving.

2 Chronicles 24:10 says:

> *"And all the princes and all the people rejoiced, and brought in, and cast into the chest, until they had made an end."*

6. **When people seek and serve the Lord, they not only want to give, but they prosper and begin giving larger offerings.**

2 Chronicles 24:11 says:

> *"Now it came to pass, that at what time the chest was brought unto the king's office by the hand of the Levites, and when they saw that there was much money, the king's scribe and the high priest's officer came and emptied the chest, and took it, and carried it to his place again. Thus they did day by day, and gathered money in abundance."*

Several kindred factors are involved in this scripture.

First, there was a lot of money ... the people gave as directed.

Second, people were giving every day and not just on Sunday.

Third, there was more than enough ... the scripture says they *"... gathered money in abundance."*

Over the years, I've heard people criticize ministries and churches because they were collecting so much money ... as if it's a bad thing when people are led to give a lot to God's work.

However, in this particular verse, it seems **that the scripture says that collecting more than enough money to meet a need was a good thing.**

7. God wants the places where people worship Him built with excellence, furnished in elegance and adorned in opulence.

"Why did that church build such a big building with all that fancy stuff in it? They should have given that money to the poor."

Have you ever heard a similar statement? I have, way too many times. If you want to know the answer, just ask God or read 2 Chronicles 24:14 which says:

> *"And when they had finished it, they brought the rest of the money before the king and Jehoiada, whereof were made vessels for the house of the*

LORD, even vessels to minister, and to offer withal, and spoons, and vessels of gold and silver. And they offered burnt offerings in the house of the LORD continually all the days of Jehoiada."

God wants things done in His house and in His name ... in a first class manner.

8. Your failure to give will keep you from prospering.

2 Chronicles 24:20 says:

"... Why transgress ye the commandments of the LORD, that ye cannot prosper? ..."

Who keeps us from prospering? We do. I realize that some may consider this a harsh statement, but when we look at all the facts ... we'll find it to be true.

The New Living Translation of this verse says:

"This is what God says: Why do you disobey the Lord's commands and keep yourselves from prospering?"

9. When people withhold their giving, God isn't too pleased about it.

The last part of 2 Chronicles 24:20 says:

"... because ye have forsaken the LORD, he hath also forsaken you ..."

The Message Bible version of the verse says:

> *"... Why have you deliberately walked away from God's commandments? You can't live this way! ..."*

Bottom line, when you are ignoring the principles God put in place, then you're ignoring Him.

10. God will bless you when you follow His instructions and give ... but if you touch His anointed, then you will die.

2 Chronicles 24:22 in the Amplified Bible says:

> *"Thus Joash the king did not remember the kindness which Jehoiada, Zechariah's father, had done him, but slew his son. And when [Zechariah the priest] was dying, he said, May the Lord see and avenge!"*

King Joash forgot that he owed his life to Jehoiada.

Even though King Joash did many wonderful things for the Lord ... he forgot that it was God who prospered him.

The list for us is simple ... always remember ... in whom you live, move and have your being (Acts 17:28).

Remember that it is God who gives you the power to get wealth (Deuteronomy 8:18) and that you should always honor those who have been your teachers, mentors and friends (Galatians 6:6).

There are a lot of things we ought to know ... but when we pay attention to these ten … we truly have the mind of God.

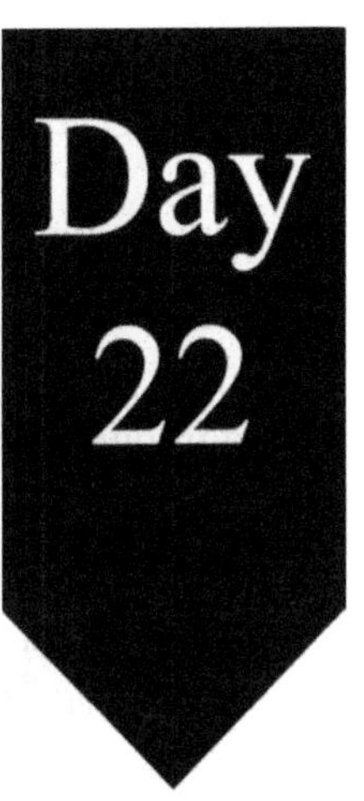

7 Things God Takes Pleasure In

Have you ever thought about what you're going to do in heaven?

Truthfully, I've never given heaven a great deal of thought since I've got a confirmed First Class ticket.

I know it's going to be glorious ... beyond my natural ability to comprehend ... I just know it's going to be glorious.

As I said, I know I'm going ...

But a few days ago my thinking got provoked when I read Revelation 2:26 in the New International Version. It says:

> *"To him who overcomes and does my will to the end, I will give authority over the nations."*

Now I've got to tell you that I got excited when I read that passage of scripture.

So I decided to read it in the Message Bible, and this is what it says:

> *"Here's the reward I have for every conqueror,*

> *everyone who keeps at it, refusing to give up: You'll rule the nations."*

By this time I was jumping out of my chair and shouting, "Shandi."

So I decided to read it in the Living Bible translation:

> *"To everyone who overcomes—who to the very end keeps on doing things that please me—I will give power over the nations."*

Can I get a witness? Are you seeing this?

You must first be an overcomer.

Romans 8:37 says:

> *"Nay, in all these things we are more than* ***conquerors*** *through him that loved us."*

In the Strong's Concordance the word conqueror is translated 24 of 28 times as "overcomer."

Here's what I know ...

First, I must be an overcomer.

Second, I must do His will as long as I draw breath on planet earth.

Third, I also must never give up.

Fourth, I must do the things that please Him.

What pleases God? In searching the scriptures He led me to seven things that give Him pleasure and a few things He's not too happy about.

1. **Our prosperity pleases God.**

Psalm 35:27 says:

> *"Let them shout for joy, and be glad, that favour my righteous cause: yea, let them say continually, Let the LORD be magnified, which hath* ***pleasure*** *in the prosperity of his servant."*

2. **When we're obedient to His divine direction, it brings Him pleasure.**

Psalm 103:21 in the Amplified Bible says:

> *"Bless (affectionately, gratefully praise) the Lord, all you His hosts, you His ministers who do His pleasure."*

God is not moved by nor does He take pleasure in people who do things through their own might and power.

Psalm 147:10 in the New Living Translation says:

> *"He takes no **pleasure** in the strength of a horse or in human might."*

The Message Bible Translation of Psalm 147:10 uses a little more contemporary analogy.

> *"He's not impressed with horsepower; the size of our muscles means little to him."*

3. **<u>God is not as much interested in what you can do but what He can do through you</u>.**

However, when we demonstrate a reverential fear of God ... it gives Him pleasure. When we want what He wants ... He can build His kingdom on earth.

Psalm 147:11 says:

> "The LORD taketh **pleasure** in them that fear him, in those that hope in his mercy."

The Message Bible translation of Psalm 147:11 says:

> ***"Those who fear God get God's attention; they can depend on his strength."***

4. **The Lord takes pleasure in the salvation of His children, and particularly the meek (humble).**

Psalm 149:4 says:

> *"For the LORD taketh* ***pleasure*** *in his people: he will beautify the meek with salvation."*

Before going any further ... let's talk about several things God definitely doesn't take pleasure in.

For instance, **God does not take pleasure in people who make vows or commitments without keeping them.**

Ecclesiastes 5:4 says:

> *"When thou vowest a vow unto God, defer not to pay it; for he hath no* ***pleasure*** *in fools: pay that which thou hast vowed."*

It's very clear from the Message Bible translation of Ecclesiastes 5:4 that **if you tell God you're going to do something ... He expects you to do it.**

> *"When you tell God you'll do something, do it—now. God takes no* ***pleasure*** *in foolish gabble. Vow it, then do it. Far better not to vow in the first place than to vow and not pay up."*

God does not take pleasure in our wickedness ... or sin. Psalm 5:4 in the New Living Translation says:

> *"O God, you take no* ***pleasure*** *in wickedness; you cannot tolerate the sins of the wicked."*

5. Do you want to be one of God's heroes ...

and I'm not taking about a television show or someone from a Marvel comic book.

You can be a superhero for God. The key is found in Psalm 16:3 in the New Living Translation:

*"The godly people in the land are my true heroes! I take **pleasure** in them!"*

Living a godly life makes you a hero to the Master of the Universe.

The Lord wants to take pleasure in all that He has created.

6. **God takes pleasure in those believers who will have the honor of living with Him forever in heaven.**

Psalm 16:11 in the New Living Translation says:

*"You will show me the way of life, granting me the joy of your presence and the **pleasures** of living with you forever."*

There is going to come a point in your life ... **when you begin to realize, understand and appreciate the source of real and lasting pleasure.**

Ecclesiastes 2:24 in the New Living Translation says:

"So I decided there is nothing better than to enjoy food and drink and to find satisfaction in work.

Then I realized that these ***pleasures*** *are from the hand of God."*

7. **If you want God to take pleasure in you ... then Proverbs 8:32-36 in the Message Bible offers some pretty sound advice.**

"So, my dear friends, listen carefully; those who embrace these my ways are most blessed. Mark a life of discipline and live wisely; don't squander your precious life. Blessed the man, blessed the woman, who listens to me, ***awake and ready for me each morning, alert and responsive*** *as I start my day's work. When you find me, you find life, real life, to say nothing of God's good* ***pleasure****. But if you wrong me, you damage your very soul; when you reject me, you're flirting with death."*

Make the most of every moment of every day. **Seek His presence ... spend time with Him ... listen to Him ... obey His divine directions.** The scripture is clear ... when we do these things, then He will give us His good pleasure.

My new goal is to live my life in such a manner that when I get to heaven ... my reward will be to rule the nations.

But truthfully, according to Psalm 2:8 in the Amplified Bible ... we don't have to wait until we get to heaven.

"Ask of Me, and I will give You the nations as Your inheritance, and the uttermost parts of the earth as Your possession."

You gotta smile when you read Psalm 2:7-8 in the Message Bible translation which says:

> *"Let me tell you what God said next. He said, 'You're my son, And today is your birthday. What do you want? Name it: Nations as a present? Continents as a prize?' "*

How do we receive nations as a present? Present the gospel to them! God says He will give them to us … just for the asking.

My heartfelt desire is for God to take pleasure in me ... because of the promises in His word ... and He knows how to throw one great birthday party.

My Heavenly Father ... is giving me the nations ... I like that. Now I just need to prove to Him that I'm a good and faithful servant to Him ... one who follows His instructions.

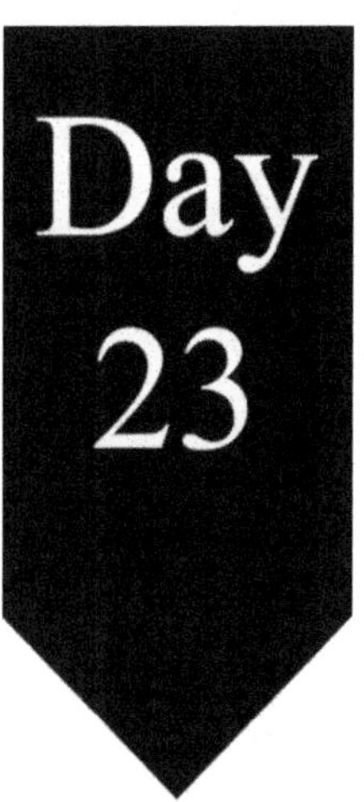

What Were You Thinking?

Now, let's be honest.

Have you ever been in a conversation where someone was going on and on and on about something you had absolutely no interest in?

Was it somebody close to you? Was it a spouse, a child, a co-worker, your boss or someone at church?

Where was your mind while they were talking?

Were you thinking about what you were going to say or do next?

Were you happy that the person doing the talking didn't really know what you were thinking?

Now let's think about that for a moment ...

Have you ever cast an admiring (lustful) glance at a person of the opposite sex ... comforted by the fact that no one could possibly know what you're thinking?

Have you ever been to a movie or watched something on a TV premium channel when nobody else was around ...

comforted once again by the illusion that nobody would know what thoughts you were allowing into your heart and mind?

If you answered “yes” to any of these questions ... then you’re one of the reasons the Lord led me to read Jeremiah 17:10 which says:

> *“I the LORD, search the heart, I try the reins, even to give every man according to his ways, and according to the fruit of his doings.”*

Now I will confess to you that I don’t often read Jeremiah, although it is a powerful book with great revelations. Truthfully, it’s mostly because it was written by a weeping prophet, and I like reading things written by happy prophets. Wait, is that an oxymoron? Just kidding; don’t get upset with me. I’m having a little fun with a moment of my Harold humor.

Here’s what I know by my personal experience and self-examination.

We have a tendency to judge other people by what they do and ourselves by what we intend to do.

I’m going to say that one more time because I want the truth of that statement to sink into your subconscious thinking.

We have a tendency to judge other people by what they do and ourselves by what we intend to do.

You and I need to fully understand that God looks at things in a totally different way.

God searches the heart. Here's a revelation ... we can't hide anything from God.

My good friend Brother Bob Harrington, the Chaplain of Bourbon Street, tells the story of a drunk who approached him early one morning just outside a bar on Bourbon Street in New Orleans.

The drunk, recognizing Brother Bob, asked him to pray for him. Brother Bob, with the typical fire that lives in his bones, said, "Lord, sober this drunk up and save him in Jesus' name."

The drunk man looked up rather startled and said, "Sshh, don't tell Him I'm drunk. Tell Him I'm sick."

That's a rather humorous but truthful illustration on how many people think God doesn't know what they do. The point is ... you and I can't hide ANYTHING from God. I mean NOTHING ... NO … THING.

The New International Version of Jeremiah 17:10 says:

> *"I the LORD search the heart and examine the mind ..."*

We CANNOT hide ANYTHING from God. He will search our hearts ... not our intentions ... but our hearts. He will examine our minds revealing what we're really thinking.

The thoughts and intents of our hearts will be laid bare.

In fact, Hebrews 4:12 says:

> *"For the word of God is quick, and powerful, and sharper than any twoedged sword, piercing even to the dividing asunder of soul and spirit, and of the joints and marrow, and* ***is a discerner of the thoughts and intents of the heart."***

I'm not going to teach on this all today ... but the phrase *dividing asunder* in this verse is the Greek word ***merismos*** (G3311).

I want to recommend a book that I read some years ago. It's entitled *Merismos* by Randy Shankle. It contains profound, thought-provoking revelations on separating the soul and the spirit.

A dear friend of mine John Daigle gave me the book with one stipulation ... that I not teach the book for one year until I had time to fully digest its contents. I agreed. In fact, I also reread that book almost every month during the remainder of that year.

During a very important season in my life ... John became a treasured mentor and remains a longtime friend. Instead of beginning a phone conversation with "Hi" or "Hello" or "What's Up" … we began our calls by saying, "Teach me something."

One more thing, *Merismos* is the only book that I've read of Mr. Shankle's. I make it a practice to never recommend a book I haven't read.

Now back to the teaching.

I particularly like the Amplified Bible translation of Hebrews 4:12 which says:

> *"For the Word that God speaks is alive and full of power [making it active, operative, energizing, and effective]; it is sharper than any two-edged sword, penetrating to the dividing line of the breath of life (soul) and [the immortal] spirit, and of joints and marrow [of the deepest parts of our nature], **exposing and sifting and analyzing and judging the very thoughts and purposes of the heart.**"*

God *"... is a discerner of the thoughts and intents of the heart."* He is *"... exposing and sifting and analyzing and judging the very thoughts and purposes of the heart."*

Bottom line again ... you can't hide anything from God.

With Hebrews 4:12 in mind ... let's look at The Message Bible translation of Jeremiah 17:10 which says:

> *"I treat them as they really are, not as they pretend to be."*

Are you beginning to get the picture?

We can't keep anything from God ... we must keep our minds pure before Him.

That's why the words of Philippians 4:8 in the Message Bible offer us a great way to keep the thoughts and intents of our hearts pure before him. The verse says:

> *"Summing it all up, friends, I'd say you'll do best by filling your minds and meditating on things true, noble, reputable, authentic, compelling, gracious—the best, not the worst; the beautiful, not the ugly; things to praise, not things to curse. Put into practice what you learned from me, what you heard and saw and realized. Do that, and God, who makes everything work together, will work you into his most excellent harmonies."*

You might be thinking, "Yes, but Brother Harold, that sounds a whole lot easier than it is." I'm not arguing that point ... you may need to change what you allow to enter your mental hard drive ... but I'm telling you it will be worth the effort.

The New International Version of Jeremiah 17:10 says:

> *"I the Lord search the heart and examine the mind, to reward each person according to their conduct, according to what their deeds deserve."*

God will REWARD YOU according to your conduct ... or as the King James Version says, **God will "... give every man according to his ways, and according to the fruit of his doings."**

The word *give* in the Strong's Concordance is the Hebrew word ***nathan*** (H5414) and it means:

"to give, bestow, grant, permit, ascribe, employ, devote, consecrate, dedicate, pay wages, sell, exchange, lend, commit, entrust, give over, deliver up, yield produce, occasion, produce, requite to, report, mention, utter, stretch out, extend."

Now, having God give to me like the scripture says ... well, that's what I call a serious reward.

If you ever needed a motivation to change the way you're thinking and what you're thinking about ... I'd say ... that's it.

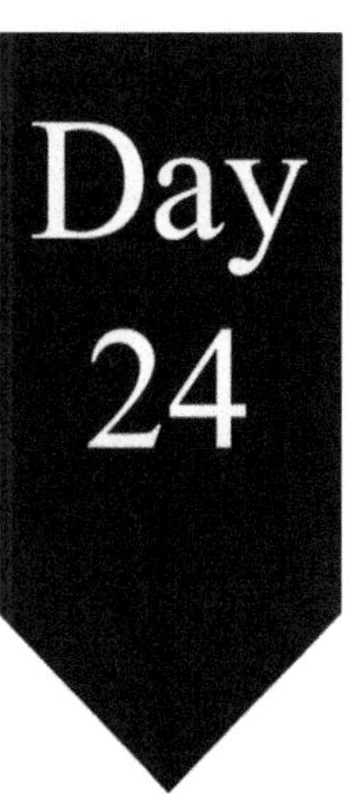

How Valuable Is Your Seed?

Your current economic circumstances determine the value of your seed. It is the most precious when it is scarce.

When the **money seed you wish to put into God's work is scarce, let your faith grow by what God says about it:**

Psalm 126:6 says:

> *"He that goeth forth and weepeth, bearing precious seed,* ***shall doubtless come again with rejoicing,*** *bringing his sheaves with him."*

That verse should give you comfort and boldness to give to God's work, even in tight financial times.

God absolutely guarantees that precious seed will produce a return; His Word says the one who sows it *"... shall doubtless come again with rejoicing ..."*

Psalm 126:6 in the Message Bible says:

> *"And now,* ***God, do it again****—bring rains to our drought-stricken lives so those who planted their crops in despair will shout hurrahs at the harvest,*

> *so those who went off with heavy hearts will come home laughing, with armloads of blessing."*

This is a favorite translation of mine because ... we will come home laughing ... with armloads of blessings.

Those who give when it isn't easy ... those who sow when it isn't convenient ... those who continue to give in the midst of lack ... will come home laughing with armloads of blessings.

Have you ever thought about how God establishes value?

Well, get in your mind first that He needs nothing.

If He has no needs, what is valuable to Him? **The cattle all belong to Him, and all the earth belongs to Him.** The universe belongs to Him. The silver is His, and the gold is His.

Everything that exists belongs to Him.

How do you establish value if you own *everything?* How much is a cow worth if you own every cow in the world? What would you give for one more cow?

Have you ever thought about how God establishes value?

In Isaiah 55:8-9 the Word says:

> *"For my thoughts are not your thoughts neither are my ways your ways, saith the Lord. For as the*

> *heavens are higher than the earth, so are my ways higher than yours and my thoughts than your thoughts."*

Jehovah God doesn't think like we think, and **He definitely doesn't establish the value of things the way we do.**

But **He does have a way of putting value on the things we give Him.**

This is a little difficult for some people to grasp, but **YESTERDAY morning in churches all over the world there WERE people that out gave Bill Gates.**

You may say, "Brother Harold, I can't believe that. I mean, Bill Gates will sometimes give a billion dollars to something."

We're **going to talk about some things that will go beyond anything you've probably ever put into your mind.** It's going to be life changing. It'll launch a whole new kind of life for you ... if you can grasp what I say next.

Mark 12:41 says:

> *"And Jesus sat over against the treasury, and beheld **how the people cast money into the treasury ..."***

Notice it **does not say that He was looking at *how much* they cast into the treasury. He was looking beyond that.**

He wasn't looking in the envelope for value, but He was looking into their hearts.

Then Mark 12:41says:

> *"... and many that were rich cast in much."*

It was "much" in the fact that there was a lot of it. I mean $1000 and $5000 checks were going in. One hundred dollar bills were falling in. Here we see a big, powerful offering taking place.

All of a sudden, Jesus makes a statement that **is totally different from the way the disciples have determined value.** A certain poor woman comes along …

Mark 12:42 says:

> *"And there came a certain poor widow, and she threw in two mites, which make a farthing."*

Now you should be careful when you read "two mites," because it's traditionally been compared to two pennies. But **two mites were equal to four Roman pennies.** A Roman soldier made sixteen pennies a day. So we find that **this woman had 25% of a Roman soldier's pay in her hand.**

And that's all she had.

Now **others *cast* their money in**, but **this woman *threw* her money in.** It's so easy to deal with finances out of your surplus, but **when you come to life-sustaining**

money, money that's at the core of your life, it gets a bit more difficult.

I can imagine her coming, **probably somewhat nervously,** thinking, ***I don't know whether I'm going to be able to do this or not.*** Then, all of a sudden, **before she could change her mind, she just threw the money in.**

This is when Jesus does something significant in Mark 12:43:

> *"And he called unto him his disciples, and saith unto them, **Verily** I say unto you, that this poor widow hath cast more in, more than all they which have cast into the treasury."*

Now, **any time we see Jesus say "Verily"** we can mark it down that **He's going to say something that people will probably have a hard time believing.**

What Jesus is saying here is, **"You're not going to understand this because you've watched the hundreds and the thousands, and that is how you determine your value.** Verily, *I* say unto you—**this poor widow has cast in more than all they which have cast into the treasury."**

Jesus didn't say what everybody else said … Jesus didn't say what public opinion says. He said:

> *"I say unto you ... **[I'm drawing a conclusion about this offering.]** Verily I say unto you, that this poor widow has cast more in, than all they which have cast into the treasury."*

Then Jesus explains Himself in Mark 12:44:

> *"For they did cast in of their abundance; but she of her want did cast in all that she had, even all her living."*

Right here in scripture, Jesus told us His value system when it comes to giving. Now that word **"*for*" is probably better understood today as "because."** Jesus tells us why the widow's offering is more valuable than all the other offerings that day.

> *"For they did cast in of their* ***abundance****; but she of her* ***want*** *did cast in all that she had, even all her living."*

That word *abundance* doesn't just mean that they had a lot. **It means there was surplus in their house.** The **bills were all paid and the cupboards were full.**

Mark 12:44 in the New Living Translation says:

> *"For they gave a tiny part of their surplus, but she, poor as she is, has given everything she had to live on."*

They gave out of that which remained *after* all of their needs were met.

Once again, let's look at Mark 12:44 in the Message Bible:

> *"All the others gave what they'll never miss; she gave extravagantly what she couldn't afford—she gave her all."*

Jesus is not looking into the envelope as much as He's looking into the heart.

When He looks into the heart, **He is not seeing what has been given as much as He's seeing what's left after the gift.** This widow woman out gave the whole crowd, not because her four mites were worth more than a thousand dollars, but because of what remained after she gave.

We may measure everything by how much the offering is, but **Jesus measures an offering by how much is left after it's given.**

That little widow set the value of her offering. She <u>set the value of it because she placed on it a dimension of value that had nothing to do with dollars and cents</u>.

Now you know what Our Heavenly Father knows ... the real value of a seed.

What Will You Do With 280?

280. What does the number 280 mean to you?

Need a hint? 280 is not money ... but then it could be ... that's your choice.

Would it surprise you to know that 280 is more valuable than money?

I'm going to resist the temptation to keep you guessing ... because I've got so much to share in this message.

280 days is about three-quarters of a year … 9 months … 40 weeks … the length of time it takes a baby to form …

Here are seven keys to prove that **what you have or have not accomplished in the first 85 days of this year will not determine what you can accomplish in the next 280 days.**

The first key is to discover what God has to say about your future.

Jeremiah 31:17 in the New Living Translation says:

> *"There is hope for your future ..."*

Personalize this verse with your name …

> *"There is hope for [Name's] future ..."*

Your Heavenly Father made a covenant with Abraham that is still as good today as it was thousands of years ago ... **God does not change His mind ... there is no expiration date on His promises.** (Numbers 23:19; Hebrews 13:8)

Deuteronomy 29:15 in the New Living Translation says:

> *"I am making this covenant both with you who stand here today in the presence of the Lord our God, and also with the future generations who are not standing here today."*

Not only do you have a covenant that's still operational ... God has plans for you.

Jeremiah 29:11 in the Contemporary English Version says:

> *"I will bless you with a future filled with hope—a future of success, not of suffering."*

Personalize this verse with your name …

> *"I will bless [Name] with a future filled with hope—a future of success, not of suffering."*

You don't have to wonder what God wants for you ... just ask Him ... get Him involved in your plan for the up-coming year ... that's the only way you'll ever succeed.

John 16:13 in the New Living Translation says:

> *"When the Spirit of truth comes, he will guide you into all truth. He will not speak on his own but will tell you what he has heard. He will tell you about the future."*

The second key is to ... develop a daily plan for the next 280 days. Refuse to take any day for granted.

I encourage you to have a plan for every day. Before you pillow your head at night, have a written plan as to what you need to accomplish the next day. Write this information out at least one hour before you lay down ... if not, your mind will begin considering possibilities for the day, and you'll find it difficult to sleep.

There is a Latin phrase that I really like ... it's called *Carpe Diem,* and it means to "Seize the Day."

Psalm 118:24 in the New Living Translation says:

> *"This is the day the Lord has made. We will rejoice and be glad in it."*

I know that you know what I'm about to say ... but I want you to ponder the ramifications of what it means ... **EVERY DAY IS A GIFT FROM GOD ... WHAT YOU DO WITH THAT DAY IS YOUR GIFT TO GOD.**

The third key is to ... believe there are no limitations to what you can achieve.

My friend John Mason says:

"Do just once what others say you can't do and you will never pay attention to their limitations again."

There is another great quote, although I'm not sure who said it: **"What would you do tomorrow if you knew you couldn't fail?"**

Job 42:2 in the Amplified Bible says:

> *"I know that You can do all things, and that no thought or purpose of Yours can be restrained or thwarted."*

The Message Bible translation of Job 42:2 says:

> *"... I'm convinced: You can do anything and everything. Nothing and no one can upset your plans."*

You have been empowered by the greatest force in the universe to achieve what others may think impossible ... but not to you.

Luke 1:37 in the Amplified Bible says:

> *"For with God nothing is ever impossible and no word from God shall be without power or impossible of fulfillment."*

The fourth key is to ... create a confession that will empower your 280-day plan.

In my teaching "7 Things To Do Before You Go To Sleep" (which you can find at haroldherring.com … search for sleep), Number 3 is **"Create a nightly confession about tomorrow being the best day of your life."**

Pray this prayer every night …

"Heavenly Father, I thank you [date] will be the greatest [day] of my life ... a day filled with revelatory insight, previously unknown opportunities, divine connections, spiritual discoveries and the ability to think beyond my imagination. My desire is for you to be glorified in everything I say and do on [day, date]. In the mighty name of Jesus. Amen."

You may choose different words ... but you need to develop a confession that fits your personality and where you are in life right now. The important point is for this confession to be as familiar to you as the air that you breathe.

Isaiah 55:11 in the Amplified Bible says:

> *"So shall My word be that goes forth out of My mouth: it shall not return to Me void [without producing any effect, useless], but it shall accomplish that which I please and purpose, and* ***it shall prosper in the thing for which I sent it."***

The fifth key is to ... monitor the plan that you've created on a daily, weekly and monthly basis.

Simply said, you must inspect what you expect … to

prevent defects … if you want to be perfect in your plan.

As I prepared this teaching I came across Lamentations 3:40 in the New Living Translation which says:

> *"Instead, let us test and examine our ways. Let us turn back to the Lord."*

In monitoring your progress ... you will find that any turning from the Lord or minimizing your time with Him ... will adversely affect your progress. That's why monitoring or self-examination is one of the most important things you can do.

1 Timothy 4:15 in the New Living Translation says:

> *"Give your complete attention to these matters. Throw yourself into your tasks so that everyone will see your progress."*

The sixth key is to ... praise God on a daily basis for the progress that you're making.

Praising God is not something that we do just on Sundays or with a "Praise God" once in a while.

Praising Him should be on a regular basis. Psalm 35:28 says:

> *"And my tongue shall speak of thy righteousness and of thy praise all the day long."*

God will give you everything He's promised you in His

Word ... just so you can praise and glorify Him.

Ephesians 1:14 in the New Living Translation says:

> *"The Spirit is God's guarantee that he will give us the inheritance he promised and that he has purchased us to be his own people. He did this so we would praise and glorify him."*

The seventh key is to ... never give up, never give in and never back down from the things that God has stirred in your spirit.

Make no mistake about it ... **the enemy will do what he thinks he can get away with to discourage and dishearten you** ... he has but one goal for the next 280 days, and that's to steal the potential God has put in you.

What should you do when these enemy attacks come? There is some pretty good advice found in Luke 18:1 in the New Living Translation:

> *"One day Jesus told his disciples a story to show that they should always pray and never give up."*

That's the best advice I can give you ... if you mess up under the heat of an attack then PRAY and NEVER GIVE UP.

One final thought … found in Ecclesiastes 5:19 in the New Living Translation:

> *"And it is a good thing to receive wealth from God*

> *and the good health to enjoy it. To enjoy your work and accept your lot in life—this is indeed a gift from God."*

God has given you 280 gifts during the next 40 weeks … the next 9 months ... what are you going to do with them? Make your Heavenly Father proud of you.

The famous entrepreneur Napoleon Hill said once, **"It's always your next move."**

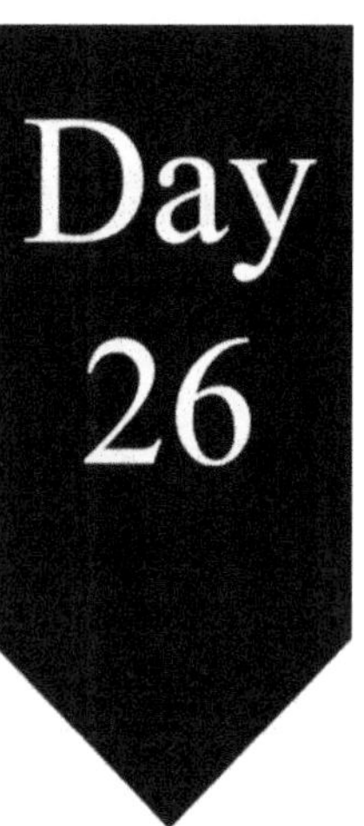

Seven Ways To Avoid God's Financial Judgment

As believers we must stop looking at where we are AND begin to anticipate and prepare themselves for where we're going to be.

If we focus all our mental energy on what we don't have instead of what we can have ... then we will forever live in shortage and lack. **Focus is a destiny breaker or maker.**

The financial choices we make today will determine our economic reality tomorrow. God has established certain economic laws ... if we violate those laws then we suffer the consequences.

Nothing is beyond the power of God. The best laid plans of men will crumble upon the trash heap of history unless directed by God.

Proverbs 21:30 in the Amplified Bible says:

> *"There is no [human] wisdom or understanding or counsel [that can prevail] against the Lord."*

What's God's plan for our money? It's the same today as it was yesterday and throughout history. It's never changed and never will.

Malachi 3:6 in the New Living Translation says:

> *"I am the Lord, and I do not change ..."*

Listen to God's directions and don't be swayed by man's opinions.

As I was reading Malachi 3 I was also stirred by Verse 5 in the Contemporary English Version which says:

> *"The LORD All-Powerful said: I'm now on my way to judge you. And I will quickly condemn all who practice witchcraft or cheat in marriage or tell lies in court or rob workers of their pay or mistreat widows and orphans or steal the property of foreigners or refuse to respect me."*

<u>God loves all of us but He judges us by what we do and don't do</u>.

This verse contains seven things that don't make God a happy camper. He judges those who:

1. **practice witchcraft**
2. **cheat in marriage**
3. **lie to authority**
4. **rob workers of pay**
5. **mistreat widows and orphans**
6. **steal the property of foreigners**
7. **refuse to respect Him**

I'm certain that most everyone reading this list is breathing a sigh of relief because they find themselves "not guilty."

The real question is not the verdict that we render on ourselves, but what does God think?

Just wondering about a few things ... let's look at these seven things one at a time.

1. Does sorcery or witchcraft have anything to do with reading horoscopes, using an Ouija board, watching movies that deal with demon possession? How about wishing evil upon another person (cursing them or casting a spell) ... how about manipulation ... just wondering.

2. Cheating in marriage ... does that refer to just the actual act of adultery? Or does it involve withholding sex or using it as a bargaining tool in marriage? How about visiting pornographic web-sites? Does your mind wander when you see an attractive, sexy actor or actress in the movies … or watching R-rated movies full of sex scenes? What about the not-so-casual glance at a member of the opposite sex? Does anything that takes your mind off your marriage partner and robs them of your affection count?

3. Just wondering about telling lies in court or to legal authorities ... does that include telling the police officer you didn't know you were speeding? How about running the stop sign or light because no one else is around? Or perhaps "fudging" on your taxes?

The King James Version says “false swearers” and the New Living Translation says “liars.” Would either of those two descriptions change your perception of how you will fare in God’s judgment of your actions?

4. Have you ever been robbed of your wages? Have you ever robbed anybody else of what was rightfully theirs? If you take anything that belongs to someone else … items they paid for with money they earned while on the job ... you have in fact robbed them of their wages. The Message Bible even talks about people who “exploit workers.”

   There are some Christians who would never knowingly steal from a person, yet they do so every time they go to a restaurant and do not properly tip their food server.

5. If I were to ask you if you mistreat widows and orphans, I’m sure the vast majority would say “absolutely not.” But here’s a question ... if God tells us to care for the widows and orphans as He does numerous times in the scripture, would lack of care be considered mistreating them ... because we haven’t done what God told us to do? Just asking.

6. I’m reasonably certain that you feel you’ve never stolen the property of foreigners. Do you employ foreign workers as domestics or laborers? Do you treat them fairly? Do you pay them under the table as an accommodation to secure assistance from someone who will work for less money to remain anonymous?

The King James Version says to *"... turn aside the stranger from his right."* The Message Bible says *"... those who are inhospitable to the homeless."* So let me ask you again ... if this applies to any of us.

7. I'm certain you would never "refuse to respect" your Heavenly Father.

   Let me ask you a question ... **if your children don't respect your instructions ... do you feel they're not respecting you?** If your children don't speak to you in a proper tone and with a right attitude, is that considered disrespect?

   The Message Bible cites *"... anyone and everyone who doesn't honor me."*

Perhaps we should think about our answers to these seven points a little more.

In the meantime, you and I can be very thankful on a number of levels for Malachi 3:7 in the Amplified Bible which says:

> *"Even from the days of your fathers you have turned aside from My ordinances and have not kept them. Return to me, and I will return to you, says the Lord of hosts. But you say, How shall we return?"*

When we return to God ... He will return to us. That's really good news. However, Verse 7 ends with a question ... how do we return to Him?

The answer is found in Malachi 3:8 which in the Amplified Bible says:

> *"Will a man rob or defraud God? Yet you rob and defraud Me. But you say, In what way do we rob or defraud You? [You have withheld your] tithes and offerings."*

Malachi 3:10 in the Amplified Bible says:

> *"Bring all the tithes (the whole tenth of your income) into the storehouse, that there may be food in My house, and prove Me now by it, says the Lord of hosts, if I will not open the windows of heaven for you and pour you out a blessing, that there shall not be room enough to receive it."*

When we honor God ... by respecting His Word ... by honoring His instructions regardless of what's happening in the nation's or world's economy ... we will be abundantly provided for by the Word economy.

While everyone else is experiencing an economic downturn you will be receive more blessings than you have room to receive.

The Message Bible says that God will *"... pour out blessings beyond your wildest dreams."*

Bottom line ... you never have to guess about God's plan for your money ... you'll never have to wonder or worry how you'll survive adverse economic conditions. **You have inside information that will cause you to survive and thrive while others are taking a dive.**

The key ... just be obedient to His Word ... He's given you the financial plan, and it's never changed ... and never will.

Pablo and Leticia from Houston wrote:

"The Spiritual Entrepreneur Information System is amazing. It combines the spiritual with the practical. You are right. The investment is minimal for the results that this program can bring to a person. It's the right kind of brainwashing. It's amazing how our thought process can hinder us or enable us to succeed."

7 Things God Does When Trouble Shows Up

If trouble comes knocking on your door ... don't answer.

I will tell you that trouble doesn't carry a hazardous warning disclaimer like a pack of cigarettes.

Trouble is ugly ... yet is often disguised as beauty ... even alluring to the eyes and the natural mind.

One more thing ... **trouble never travels alone ... it's often accompanied by deceit, temptation, guilt, anxiety and, of course, sin.** They all like to party together ... with you paying the bill.

I recently shared "7 Things To Do When Trouble Comes." Today, we're going to discuss seven things God does when trouble shows up, and it's based on Psalm 138:7-8 in the New Living Translation.

> *"Though I am surrounded by troubles, you will protect me from the anger of my enemies. You reach out your hand, and the power of your right hand saves me. The Lord will work out his plans for my life—for your faithful love, O Lord, endures forever. Don't abandon me, for you made me."*

1. God protects us from the anger of our enemies.

If we're in trouble ... some of us would call for the Navy Seals ... a lean mean fighting machine with the skill set and training to vanquish any natural foe.

However, there is another force that always has the latest intel, the greatest weaponry, the tactical advantage and a track record of winning every fight. This powerful force is available to every born-again believer ... it's our great God Jehovah. Elohim, the Almighty One.

There are dozens of scriptures which prove God will protect you from every attack of the enemy, but I'm only going to share three with you.

First, Exodus 23:22 in the Amplified Bible says:

> *"But if you will indeed listen to and obey His voice ... I will be an enemy to your enemies and an adversary to your adversaries."*

Personalize it this way:

> *"But if [Name] will indeed listen to and obey His voice ... I will be an enemy to [his/her] enemies and an adversary to [his/her] adversaries."*

Second, Romans 8:31 in the Amplified Bible says:

> *"... if God is for us, who [can be] against us? [Who can be our foe, if God is on our side?]"*

Personalize it this way:

> *"... if God is for [Name], who [can be] against [him/her]? [Who can be [Name's] foe, if God is on [his/her] side?]"*

Third, Psalm 118:6 in the Message Bible says:

> *"God's now at my side and I'm not afraid; who would dare lay a hand on me?"*

Personalize this verse:

> *"God's now at [Name]'s side and [he/she] is not afraid; who would dare lay a hand on [Name]?"*

No super hero could protect any better than the Holy Spirit.

2. God wants us to reach out to Him.

In times of trouble ... if you reach out to Him ... He will reach out to you.

2 Chronicles 15:2 in the Amplified Bible says:

> *"... the Lord is with you while you are with Him. If you seek Him [inquiring for and of Him, craving Him as your soul's first necessity], He will be found by you; but if you [become indifferent and] forsake Him, He will forsake you."*

Jeremiah 29:12-14 in the Amplified Bible says:

> *"Then you will call upon Me, and you will come and pray to Me, and I will hear and heed you. Then you will seek Me, inquire for, and require Me [as a vital necessity] and find Me when you search for Me with all your heart. I will be found by you, says the Lord, and I will release you from captivity ..."*

Years ago, Southern Bell had a slogan that said, "Reach out, and we'll be there."

When you call upon the Lord ... that's one customer service call you'll never have to worry about again.

3. God saves us.

"Amazing grace, how sweet the sound ... that saved a wretch like me."

The first line of *Amazing Grace* says it all.

It was by His grace ... unmerited favor ... that I was positioned to receive and accept my salvation.

I didn't earn it ... couldn't buy it ... win it ... inherit it ... but it's mine ... simply because at the LaGrange Free Will Baptist Church in North Carolina ... a little boy walked the aisle and asked Jesus into His heart.

The great news is God not only saves our souls ... but He saves us in so many other ways.

Matthew 14:30-31 in the Amplified Bible says:

> *"But when he perceived and felt the strong wind, he was frightened, and as he began to sink, he cried out, Lord, save me [from death]! Instantly Jesus reached out His hand and caught and held him, saying to him, O you of little faith, why did you doubt?"*

When you stumble and fall ... He will instantly reach out His hand to save you.

4. God works out plans for our lives.

If your life is filled with trouble, regret and confusion ... go into the Home Improvement business with God ... allow Him to renovate your interior, revealing His plans for your life. And with God's Home Improvement plan, your exterior look will begin to change to mimic your interior renovation.

When God is finished with you ... **your friends and family won't recognize you because of the improvements He's made in you.**

God's desire for you is found in Psalm 20:4 in the New Living Translation which says:

> *"May he grant your heart's desires and make all your plans succeed."*

Make no mistake … God wants you to succeed ... so much so ... that He tells you exactly how to do it.

Proverbs 16:3 in the New Living Translation says:

> *"Commit your actions to the Lord, and your plans will succeed."*

Hallelujah!!

5. God loves us faithfully.

There was a popular song some years ago entitled *What's Love Got To Do With It.*

Love has everything to do with keeping you protected from trouble and harm.

When it comes to love ... there are only two scriptures you really need to know and understand completely.

First, John 3:16 says:

> *"For God so loved the world, that he gave his only begotten Son, that whosoever believeth in him should not perish, but have everlasting life."*

Second, Matthew 22:37-39 in the Amplified Bible says:

> *"And He replied to him, You shall love the Lord your God with all your heart and with all your soul and with all your mind (intellect). This is the great (most important, principal) and first commandment. And a second is like it: You shall love your neighbor as [you do] yourself."*

6. God never abandons us.

At one time or another in your life ... you may have been abandoned by a parent, a spouse, your children, family or friends ... but there's One who will NEVER abandon you.

Never ... ever ... will He abandon you.

Deuteronomy 31:6 in the New Living Translation says:

> *"So be strong and courageous! Do not be afraid and do not panic before them. For the Lord your God will personally go ahead of you. He will neither fail you nor abandon you."*

Hebrews 13:5 in the New Living Translation says:

> *"Don't love money; be satisfied with what you have. For God has said, 'I will never fail you. I will never abandon you.' "*

7. He made us for a purpose.

When trouble comes ... sometimes the enemy also attacks our self-worth trying to make us feel that we're of no value.

Well, he's a liar, the father of lies and the truth is not in him.

I want you to get this down in your spirit. YOU ARE NOT AN ACCIDENT. You are not a mistake. God knew you before you were ever born … thought of or conceived.

Jeremiah 1:5 in the Amplified Bible says:

> *"Before I formed you in the womb I knew [and] approved of you [as My chosen instrument], and before you were born I separated and set you apart, consecrating you; [and] I appointed you as a prophet to the nations."*

Your birth parents may call you illegitimate ... but you're not. God made you for a purpose.

One last thing. It's important to realize that trouble always brings change. **Your actions and reactions will determine the kind of change that you will experience**.

13 Reasons It's Good To Have Money

Sadly, there are people who are so sure they are right in their "thinking" that they want to make every single scripture fit their own ideas.

There are those who find it difficult ... no, impossible would be a better word choice, to recognize any scripture that encourages biblical prosperity.

One of those scriptures is 1 Timothy 6:18-19.

Let's go in for a little deeper study of this verse. In fact, we're going to examine the verse in three different translations plus determine what the various words mean in Strong's Exhaustive Concordance Dictionary.

Now stay with me on this ... because if or when your well-meaning friends come against the scriptural truth of prosperity ... you need to know the facts.

As a side note, we would all be so much better off if we just seek the truth of God's Word.

If we are not open to letting God change our minds, we are in for some serious deception and real unhappiness in our lives.

1 Timothy 6:18 in the King James Version says:

> *"That they do good, that they be rich in good works, ready to distribute, willing to communicate."*

In Strong's Concordance the word *good* is the Greek word ***agathoergeō*** (G14) and it means:

"to work good, to do good, to do well, act rightly."

In Strong's Concordance the word *rich* is the Greek word ***plouteō*** (G4147) and it means:

"to be rich, to have abundance; outward possessions; to be richly supplied."

The second time the word *good* is mentioned in 1 Timothy 6:18, it's the Greek word Strong's Concordance lists as ***kalos*** (G2570) and it means:

"beautiful, handsome, excellent, eminent, choice, surpassing, precious, useful, suitable, commendable, admirable."

The word *works* is the Greek word ***ergon*** (G2041) and it means:

"business, employment, that which any one is occupied; any product whatever, anything accomplished by hand, art, industry, or mind."

Now let's look at 1 Timothy 6:19:

> *"Laying up in store for themselves a good foundation against the time to come, that they may lay hold on eternal life."*

The Greek word for *store* is ***apothēsaurizō*** (G597) and it means:

"to put away, lay by in store, to treasure away; to store up abundance for future use."

In the New Living Translation, 1Timothy 6:18-19 says:

> *"Tell them to use their money to do good. They should be rich in good works and generous to those in need, always being ready to share with others. By doing this they will be storing up their treasure as a good foundation for the future so that they may experience true life."*

What does the Word say qualifies as using our "money to do good"?

Here are **thirteen scriptural *good* things you should do with your money.**

1. Tithe.

Deuteronomy 26:11-12 says:

> *"And thou shalt rejoice in every good thing which the Lord thy God hath given unto thee, and unto*

thine house ... When thou hast made an end of tithing all the tithes of thine increase ..."

2. Fulfill the Great Commission.

Matthew 28:19-20 says:

"Go ... teach all nations, baptizing them in the name of the Father, and of the Son, and of the Holy Ghost: Teaching them to observe all things whatsoever I have commanded you: and, lo, I am with you always, even unto the end of the world. Amen."

3. Help create a better-than-average standard of living for your pastor.

1 Timothy 5:17-18 says:

"Let the elders that rule well be counted worthy of double honor, especially they who labor in the word and doctrine. For the scripture saith, Thou shalt not muzzle the ox that treadeth out the corn. And, The laborer is worthy of his reward."

Galatians 6:6 in the Living Bible says:

"Those who are taught the Word of God should help their teachers by paying them."

4. Provide for your own family.

1 Timothy 5:8 says:

> *"... if any provide not for his own, and especially for those of his own house, he hath denied the faith, and is worse than an infidel."*

5. Give good gifts to your children.

Matthew 7:11 says:

> *"If ye then, being evil, know how to give good gifts unto your children, how much more shall your Father which is in heaven give good things ...?"*

6. Have a good savings account.

Deuteronomy 28:1, 5 says:

> *"... it shall come to pass, if thou shalt harken diligently unto the voice of the Lord thy God, to observe and to do all his commandments ... Blessed shall be thy basket and thy store."*

7. Have a proper retirement account.

Proverbs 6:6-8 says:

> *"Go to the ant, thou sluggard; consider her ways, and be wise ... Which having no guide, overseer, or ruler ... Provideth her meat in the summer, and gathereth her food in the harvest."*

8. Pay all your bills in a timely manner.

Romans 13:8 in the Amplified Bible says:

> *"Keep out of debt and owe no man anything, except to love one another; for he who loves his neighbor [who practices loving others] has fulfilled the Law [relating to one's fellowmen, meeting all its requirements]."*

9. Pay your taxes.

Matthew 22:21 says:

> *"... Render therefore unto Caesar the things which are Caesar's ..."*

10. You should never have to borrow to live day to day.

Luke 16:13 says:

> *"No servant can serve two masters: for either he will hate the one, and love the other; or else he will hold to the one, and despise the other. Ye cannot serve God and mammon."*

Compare this verse to Proverbs 22:7 which says:

> *"... the borrower is servant to the lender."*

11. Give generously to the poor.

Proverbs 19:17 says:

"He that hath pity upon the poor lendeth unto the Lord; and that which he hath given will he pay him again."

12. Help those who need your assistance.

Deuteronomy 15:7, 8 and 11 says:

"If there be among you a poor man of one of thy brethren within any of thy gates in thy land which the Lord thy God giveth thee, thou shalt not harden thy heart, not shut thine hand from thy poor brother:

"But thou shalt open thine hand wide unto him, and shalt surely lend him sufficient for his need, in that which he wanteth.

"For the poor shall never cease out of the land: therefore I command thee, saying, Thou shalt open thine hand wide unto thy brother, to thy poor, and to thy needy, in thy land."

13. Care for the widows and orphans.

James 1:27 in the Contemporary English Version says:

"Religion that pleases God the Father must be pure and spotless. You must help needy orphans and widows and not let this world make you evil."

Now you know at least thirteen reasons why it's good that you have money.

Let me ask you a question ... **how many of those thirteen good things could you do effectively if you were broke?**

Now let's look at 1 Timothy 6:18-19 in the Message Bible translation:

> *"Tell them to go after God, who piles on all the riches we could ever manage—to do good, to be rich in helping others, to be extravagantly generous. If they do that, they'll build a treasury that will last, gaining life that is truly life."*

I don't really need to comment on this verse ... **it's self-explanatory and should convince any remaining skeptics.** Let's read it one more time.

> *"Tell them to go after God,* ***who piles on all the riches we could ever manage—to do good, to be rich in helping others, to be extravagantly generous.*** *If they do that, they'll build a treasury that will last, gaining life that is truly life."*

God says what He means and means what He says. There is no equivocation. I just love the Word of God. Reading the promises and instructions of 1 Timothy 6:18-19 just makes my day.

Search out Tony Compolo on YouTube. You'll find that …

If you've been arrested by debt, betrayed by creditors,

crushed by payments and deceived by lustful desires … It's Friday ... but Sunday's coming. It's time to loose the Resurrection Power of God in your personal finances.

Day 29

7 Ways To Fight Back in an Attack

Do you feel overwhelmed with attacks against your family, finances, future and health?

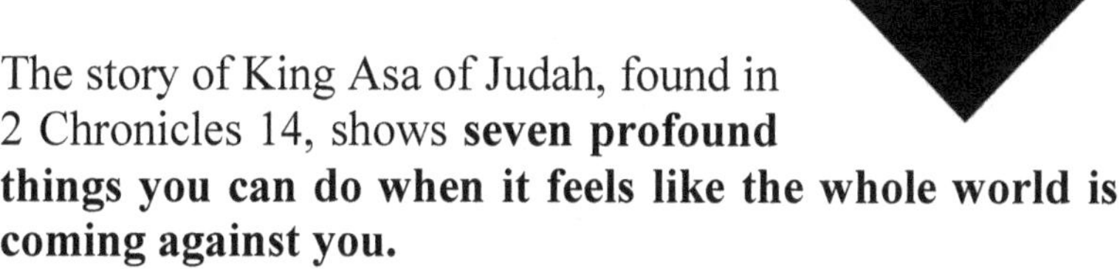

The story of King Asa of Judah, found in 2 Chronicles 14, shows **seven profound things you can do when it feels like the whole world is coming against you.**

First, you need to understand that **just because you are doing what is right in God's sight doesn't mean you won't get attacked.** It's how we respond when we are attacked that defines who we are and the degree of our success. This is a powerful story with seven powerful lessons we can apply to our lives today.

1. You must do what's right in the eyes of the Lord.

[2] "And Asa did that which was good and right in the eyes of the Lord his God ... "

You can't live like the devil all week and think being an angel in church on Sunday is going to make everything all right. **You don't have to be perfect, but your heart must be striving to be.** And make no mistake, God knows your heart.

2. **Put aside every "thing" that seeks to exalt itself above your love for God and doing His Word.**

[3] "For he took away the altars of the strange gods, and the high places, and brake down the images, and cut down the groves ... "

Idols are not just made of wood, stone and gold. Idols can include putting family, a job, house, car, clothes or anything else above God.

Everything in your life takes second place to your personal relationship with the Lord.

When your priorities are right, all those other things will actually improve with less effort anyway.

3. **Seek His presence while desiring a close relationship with him.**

[4] "And commanded Judah to seek the Lord God of their fathers, and to do the law and the commandment."

God wants to answer prayers, but a close relationship is not laying out personal needs and spiritual shopping lists.

Let His Word speak to you, and then do the things that He directs you to do.

4. <u>Get your eyes off your circumstances</u>.

[8] "And Asa had an army of men ... out of Judah three hundred thousand; and out of Benjamin ... two hundred and fourscore thousand: all these were mighty men of valour.

[9] "And there came out against them Zerah the Ethiopian with an host of a thousand thousand [that equals a million people!], and three hundred chariots ...

[10] "Then Asa went out against him, and they set the battle in array in the valley ..."

Don't let fear of what you perceive the situation to be create panic and doubt in your heart.

It may feel like your creditors are carpooling to your house, but your Heavenly Father, your Jehovah Jireh, can deliver you from every attack.

5. Get before the Lord in prayer and <u>activate the host of heaven to fight your battles</u>.

[11] "And Asa cried unto the Lord his God, and said, Lord, it is nothing with thee to help, whether with many, or with them that have no power: help us, O Lord our God; for we rest on thee, and in thy name we go against this multitude. O Lord, thou art our God; let not man prevail against thee."

What a prayer he prayed in the sight of certain defeat in

the natural! Here he had a small army compared to the million warriors he was facing.

You may feel like you're facing overwhelming odds, but the battle is not yours; it's the Lord's (2 Chronicles 20:15).

King Asa chose to believe that if God was for Him, who could be against him (Romans 8:31).

When the bills keep piling up, the creditors keep calling or there just doesn't seem to be enough money to cover all your bills … remember that **you're not in the battle alone.**

When you put your confidence in the Lord, claim His promises, confess His Word and manifest the God-kind of faith, then victory is at hand.

Be encouraged by the story of King Asa and look what happened in Verse 12:

6. Always remember who your source is!

[12] "So the Lord smote the Ethiopians before Asa and before Judah; and the Ethiopians fled. King Asa won a major victory."

Once you gain the victory, give God the glory that's due Him. Let your praise come up as a reminder of His faithfulness to you.

But beware you don't get comfortable and stop relying on the Lord as King Asa did.

Almost every day, I talk with believers who've gotten out of debt only to find they are back in … deeper than before.

I think many times believers forget "Who brought them out." In other words, success can bring complacency.

There have been times in all our lives when the only thing we've had to rely on is God. We've read, prayed and trusted. We gave as He directed, and we were delivered, but again found ourselves with one nostril above the financially troubled waters.

As Paul Harvey would say, "Here's the rest of the story" of King Asa.

Years later, the king of Israel came out against Asa. But, by this time, Asa had been a king for some time. He figured he could handle the situation himself without consulting God like he had when the Ethiopians attacked. So he used his resources to hire a worldly force (Syria) and, although he was able to defeat Israel through natural means, it didn't please God.

In 2 Chronicles 16:7-8 ... the prophet came to him and said:

> *[7] "... Because thou hast relied on the king of Syria, and not relied on the Lord thy God, therefore is the host of the king of Syria escaped out of thine hand.*
>
> *[8] "Were not the Ethiopians ... a huge host, with*

> *very many chariots and horsemen? yet, because thou didst rely on the Lord, he delivered them into thine hand."*

7. **Keep your heart focused on pleasing the Lord and He will show Himself strong on your behalf.**

2 Chronicles 16:9 says:

> *"For the eyes of the Lord run to and fro throughout the whole earth, to shew himself strong in the behalf of them whose heart is perfect toward him ..."*

King Asa forgot who brought him out. He forgot the Holy One who delivered him from his enemies.

I want you to know that your situation might look overwhelming to the natural eye, BUT GOD is not moved by circumstances.

Just as David had his Goliath and Asa faced a million Ethiopians, we have to know that God will show Himself strong on behalf of those whose hearts are leaned—with faithful assurance—toward Him.

By our attitudes and our work ethics, we will determine whether we win or lose the battles of life. No matter how great the forces arrayed against you, God is on your side.

Remember what the lyrics to *God Didn't Bring Us This Far to Leave Us* say:

God didn't bring us this far to leave us.
He didn't teach us to swim to let us drown.
He didn't build His home in us to move away.
He didn't build us up to let us down.

But you must stay focused on your faith in our righteous God who delivers us from evil, who brings us through the fire and into a wealthy place (Psalm 66:12).

I'd like to finish by reading Psalm 66:12 in the World English Bible to you. (paraphrased and personalized)

"You allowed others to ride over [Name]'s head; [Name] went through the fire and the water; but You brought [Name] to a place of abundance.

"[Name] will come into your presence with offerings.

"[Name] will pay [his/her] vows to You. Which [his/her] lips promised,

"And [his/her] mouth spoke, when [he/she] was in distress.

"[Name] will bring [his/her] offerings to You.

"The fragrance of [Name]'s offerings will rise before you."

Think of this verse as you fill in your name. In Psalm 66:18, the Word tells us if we regard iniquity in our hearts, the Lord will not hear us.

Praise God … that's the end of another excellent teaching … and God wants you immersed in his Rich Thoughts and excellent blessings!

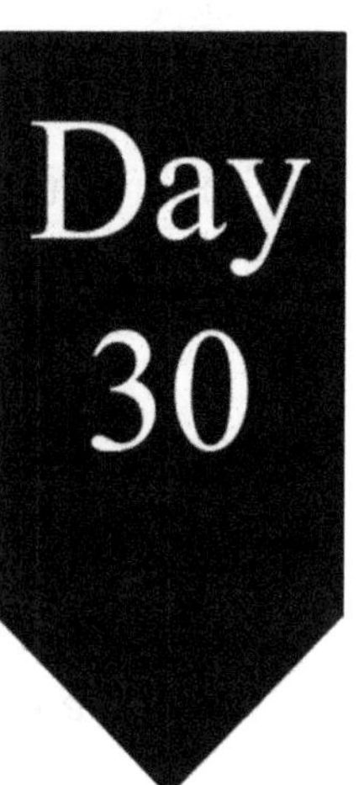

7 Things to Sow That You Also Want To Reap

Years ago there was a saying that ... I felt defined my life. It said:

"There is a destiny that makes us brothers, none goes his way alone.

"All that you pass into the lives of others will surely come back into your own."

I had this quote on my letterhead and memo pads ... it was my motivation.

I was recently reminded of this quote as I was reading Matthew 7:12:

> *"Therefore all things whatsoever ye would that men should do to you, do ye even so to them: for this is the law and the prophets."*

Here are **seven things you sow that you definitely want to reap**.

1. Love others.

I'm sure you've probably encountered people who you

don't particularly like or want to be around.

It's important to understand how God feels about others. You may not like them but you must love them ... in that, you have a command with no choice.

Matthew 22:38-39 in the Amplified Bible says:

> *"This is the great (most important, principal) and first commandment. And a second is like it: You shall love your neighbor as [you do] yourself."*

There is scripture after scripture that talks about how we should love our fellow man. Those scriptures don't say to love them if we like them ... no, they say we're to love them because we represent God on this earth.

Rather than list all the scriptures with an admonition to love one another I've decided to share one which sums it up.

1 Thessalonians 4:9 in the New Living Translation says:

> *"But we don't need to write to you about the importance of loving each other, for God himself has taught you to love one another."*

2. Believe the best about others.

One of the greatest benefits and blessings you can ever offer to another person is to believe in them.

I have something that sadly millions of believers never had

or have. I have people who believe in me.

My Mom and Dad always believed in me ... even during one of the most difficult times in my life ... they still believed in me.

My fine wife, Bev, believes in me ... even when I gave her reasons not to ... she still did.

I'm so blessed that thousands of partners believe in what God has me doing on planet earth ... as I fulfill the vision that He has given to me.

Now, you may not have had a mom, dad or spouse to believe in you, but you have someone very important who does ... that always will ... it's your Heavenly Father.

2 Corinthians 7:4 in the New Living Translation says:

> *"I have the highest confidence in you, and I take great pride in you. You have greatly encouraged me and made me happy despite all our troubles."*

3. Forgive others so they can forgive.

A friend is not necessarily someone who always does everything right. It's not necessarily one who never hurts you unintentionally, or perhaps even intentionally.

I'm not advocating that you live in toxic relationships ... but I am saying that you must forgive those who do you wrong and move on.

If someone has a pattern of continually hurting you then you need to move on or develop other friendships. But you can and must not harbor unforgiveness in your life ... to protect yourself.

Unforgiveness is bad for your scriptural and medical well-being. It actually doesn't appear in any versions of the Bible I'm most familiar with.

However, the word forgiveness appears in all four gospels from seven to sixteen times.

Matthew 18:21-22 says:

> *"Then came Peter to him, and said, Lord, how oft shall my brother sin against me, and I forgive him? till seven times? Jesus saith unto him, I say not unto thee, Until seven times: but, Until seventy times seven."*

The Message Bible says:

> *" '... how many times do I forgive a brother or sister who hurts me? Seven?' Jesus replied, 'Seven! Hardly. Try seventy times seven.' "*

In fact, what Jesus said was to make that seventy times seven every day.

Luke 17:4 in the New Living Translation says:

> *"Even if that person wrongs you seven times a day and each time turns again and asks forgiveness,*

you must forgive."

4. Advise and support others.

When you offer sound advice to others ... when you support them ... when you sow kind seeds into others, you will reap a harvest of the same. As long as the earth remains ... what you sow you will reap.

The poet Ralph Waldo Emerson, when meeting people, was prone to ask, "What have you learned since we last met?"

I think every Christian should greet one another by saying, "What has the Lord revealed to you since we last spoke?"

I have a particular friend with whom I share the same telephone greeting on every call. Instead of saying, "Hello," we greet each other with: "Teach me something."

Proverbs 1:5 says:

> *"A wise man will hear, and will increase learning; and a man of understanding shall attain unto wise counsels."*

5. Pray for others.

Praying for one another isn't just a good idea ... it's a God idea.

James 5:16 says:

> *"Confess your faults one to another, and pray one*

for another, that ye may be healed. The effectual fervent prayer of a righteous man availeth much."

The Amplified Bible translation of James 5:16 says:

"Confess to one another therefore your faults (your slips, your false steps, your offenses, your sins) and pray [also] for one another, that you may be healed and restored [to a spiritual tone of mind and heart]. The earnest (heartfelt, continued) prayer of a righteous man makes tremendous power available [dynamic in its working]."

6. Bless others.

1 Peter 3:8-9 in the Message Bible says:

"No retaliation. No sharp-tongued sarcasm. Instead, bless—that's your job, to bless. ***You'll be a blessing and also get a blessing."***

When you bless someone else ... God will bless you. In essence, whatever good thing you cause to happen to someone else ... God will do the same thing for you (Ephesians 6:8).

God wants to prosper you … so you can bless others with your generosity.

2 Corinthians 9:8 in the Amplified Bible says:

"And God is able to make all grace (every favor and earthly blessing) come to you in abundance, so

that you may always and under all circumstances and whatever the need be self-sufficient [possessing enough to require no aid or support and furnished in abundance for every good work and charitable donation]."

7. Encourage others.

Job 16:5 in the Amplified Bible says:

"[But] I would strengthen and encourage you with [the words of] my mouth, and the consolation of my lips would soothe your suffering."

We should always speak a word in season to lift up others ... to bless them. Such a lifestyle will require us to be filled with the love of God ... because it is not always easy.

If you're obedient to God's divine directives you will find yourself being sent to encourage others.

Ephesians 6:21-22 in the Amplified Bible says:

"Now that you may know how I am and what I am doing, Tychicus, the beloved brother and faithful minister in the Lord [and His service], will tell you everything.

"I have sent him to you for this very purpose, that you may know how we are and that he may console and cheer and encourage and strengthen your hearts."

If you apply these seven scriptural principles, you will become the personification of Matthew 7:12 in the Message Bible translation which says:

> *"Here is a simple, rule-of-thumb guide for behavior: Ask yourself what you want people to do for you, then grab the initiative and do it for them. Add up God's Law and Prophets and this is what you get."*

If the Bible says we will be known by our love for one another, this question is one worth repeating today: If you were arrested for being a Christian, would there enough evidence to convict you?

And … are we sowing what we want to be reaping?

RichThoughts for Breakfast
Volume 3

Invite Harold Herring to speak at your church, event, or rally.

Would you like to invite Harold to be a guest speaker at your church, event, or rally? Just send an email to:

booking@haroldherring.com

or call 1-800-583-2963

With a mix of humor, practical strategies, and Biblical insight Harold will inspire, encourage, and prepare you to change your financial destiny and set you on the path to not only set you free from debt but keep you free of debt and living the debt free life God has called you to.

Keep Thinking Rich Thoughts,

Harold Herring

www.ingramcontent.com/pod-product-compliance
Lightning Source LLC
Chambersburg PA
CBHW060305100426
42742CB00011B/1876

* 9 7 8 0 9 7 6 3 6 6 8 3 6 *